William Damon, *Brown University*
EDITOR-IN-CHIEF

Childhood Gender Segregation: Causes and Consequences

Campbell Leaper
University of California, Santa Cruz

EDITOR

Number 65, Fall 1994

JOSSEY-BASS PUBLISHERS
San Francisco

CHILDHOOD GENDER SEGREGATION: CAUSES AND CONSEQUENCES
Campbell Leaper (ed.)
New Directions for Child Development, no. 65
William Damon, Editor-in-Chief

Microfilm copies of issues and articles are available in 16mm and 35mm, as well as microfiche in 105mm, through University Microfilms Inc., 300 North Zeeb Road, Ann Arbor, Michigan 48106-1346.

LC 85-644581   ISSN 0195-2269   ISBN 0-7879-9985-7

NEW DIRECTIONS FOR CHILD DEVELOPMENT is part of The Jossey-Bass Education Series and is published quarterly by Jossey-Bass Inc., Publishers, 350 Sansome Street, San Francisco, California 94104-1342 (publication number USPS 494-090). Second-class postage paid at San Francisco, California, and at additional mailing offices. POSTMASTER: Send address changes to Jossey-Bass Inc., Publishers, 350 Sansome Street, San Francisco, California 94104-1342.

EDITORIAL CORRESPONDENCE should be sent to the Editor-in-Chief, William Damon, Department of Education, Box 1938, Brown University, Providence, Rhode Island 02912.

Cover photograph by Wernher Krutein/PHOTOVAULT © 1990.

Manufactured in the United States of America. Nearly all Jossey-Bass books, jackets, and periodicals are printed on recycled paper that contains at least 50 percent recycled waste, including 10 percent postconsumer waste. Many of our materials are also printed with vegetable-based inks; during the printing process these inks emit fewer volatile organic compounds (VOCs) than petroleum-based inks. VOCs contribute to the formation of smog.

CONTENTS

EDITOR'S NOTES

Throughout childhood, peer relations transpire predominantly within the context of same-sex peer groups (Maccoby, 1990). Therefore, girls and boys have been described as developing in different "gender cultures," because each gender group generally establishes and maintains different norms for social interaction (Carter, 1987; Maccoby and Jacklin, 1987; Maltz and Borker, 1982; Thorne and Luria, 1986). This volume—which grew out of the symposium "The Development of Gender and Relationships" that I chaired at the 1991 conference of the Society for Research in Child Development—explores ways in which these different peer environments may lead to the development of corresponding differences in individuals' psychological preferences and skills. Prior to introducing the individual chapters, however, I offer a preliminary caveat. This volume's concern with gendered peer relations and their developmental implications requires chapter authors to highlight gender differences rather than similarities. As in any comparison, there is the risk of overemphasizing the extent of differences simply by calling attention to them (Hare-Mustin and Marecek, 1988; Leaper, 1993). Thus, one limitation of the gender cultures approach is that similarities between girls and boys tend to be ignored (Thorne, 1993). For example, it is possible that the ongoing redefinitions of gender roles in some segments of society are being reflected in children's peer relations (Beverly I. Fagot, personal communication, June 11, 1993). At the same time, ignoring or minimizing those gender differences that do exist is not a satisfactory solution because it leads us to neglect an important dimension along which people's life experiences vary across the world (Hare-Mustin and Marecek, 1988; Whiting and Edwards, 1988). Moreover, even when particular children do not themselves act in sex-typed ways, they are part of a larger culture that regularly creates divergent life experiences for males and females. As the contributors to this volume argue, the phenomenon of gender segregation makes these divergent experiences especially pervasive during childhood.

There are four important questions a developmental psychologist can ask about gender segregation in children's peer relations: First, why does gender segregation occur? Second, how is it maintained? Third, what are the correlates of gender-segregated peer groups? And fourth, what are the consequences of childhood gender segregation on individuals' later psychological development? *Childhood Gender Segregation: Causes and Consequences* addresses all these questions. The question of possible developmental precursors for gender segregation is addressed by Lisa A. Serbin and her colleagues and Richard A. Fabes and Carol Lynn Martin. Processes involved in the maintenance of gender segregation are considered by Martin, Beverly I. Fagot, and myself. And both Fagot and I explore the correlates and consequences of gender-segregated peer groups. Finally, Eleanor E. Maccoby addresses all four questions in a concluding overview.

More specifically, in Chapter One, Lisa Serbin, Lora Moller, Judith Gulko, Kimberly Powlishta, and Karen Colburne present evidence in support of the behavioral compatibility hypothesis for the emergence of gender segregation. According to this explanation, originally advanced by Goodenough (1934) and Parten (1932), children of the same gender may prefer one another because they are more compatible in social interactional styles. Serbin and her colleagues support this hypothesis with their research data, presenting evidence that children generally prefer others with similar behavioral styles and suggesting that, because many differences in behavioral style are correlated with gender, early behavioral preferences may provide children's initial motivation to affiliate with same-sex peers. For example, boys tend to prefer more rough and domineering interaction styles whereas girls tend to prefer more polite and conflict-mitigating styles (Maccoby, 1990). Consequently, girls and boys may come to avoid one another because they do not like each other's style of interaction.

The research of Serbin and her colleagues still leaves open the question of why girls and boys often differ in their interactional styles. In Chapter Two, Richard Fabes argues that these gender differences may be due to underlying sex differences in emotional reactivity. He builds on Gottman and Levenson's (1988) research with adults suggesting that, during conflicts, males tend to have a higher autonomic responsivity than do females. Fabes's preliminary evidence indicates that boys may have more difficulty than girls regulating their emotional arousal, and this may contribute to boys' tendency to assert power in interactions. Interestingly, Fabes also presents results that suggest that gender differences in emotional reactivity may depend on the type of situation being observed. This finding is consistent with recent ecological models (for example, Huston, 1985) that emphasize the importance of context in the manifestation of gender-related differences.

Whereas the first two chapters examine how behavioral and affective processes may be involved in the development of gender segregation, Chapter Three, by Carol Martin, considers the role of cognitive processes. Martin notes that researchers have not established a clear link between gender-related cognitions (for example, knowledge of gender stereotypes) and the emergence of gender segregation. However, she goes on to suggest that these studies do not necessarily refute the influence of cognitive factors in the formation of same-gender peer preferences, and she presents evidence that simply acquiring a basic concept of gender (an in-group schema) may be sufficient to motivate children to be with others "like me." Specific knowledge about what it means to be a boy or a girl may follow later. Therefore, the criteria for gender stereotyping used in previous efforts to test the link between cognitive factors and the emergence of gender segregation may have been too stringent. Moreover, Martin finds that gender cognitions may play an especially important role in the maintenance and elaboration of same-sex peer preferences.

In addition to studying the developmental precursors of gender segregation, researchers have also been concerned with its possible impact on children's ongoing development. In Chapter Four, Beverly Fagot addresses some of the contemporaneous correlates and possible consequences of children's gendered peer relations. She reviews research that lends support to Block's (1983) proposal that differences in girls' and boys' playgroups and play activities contribute to the development of later gender differences in psychological skills, and presents evidence from her longitudinal data indicating that children's preferences for sex-typed play activities emerge between the second and third year. She then links children's sex-typed play to gender differences in cognitive development. Fagot's observations are compatible with other investigations emphasizing the potential impact of gender segregation on children's academic achievement (see Cherry-Wilkinson and Marrett, 1985; Liss, 1983; Lloyd and Duveen, 1992; and Lockheed and Klein, 1985, for further consideration of this topic).

In Chapter Five, I also consider the possible consequences of gender segregation on psychological development as I examine some of the ways in which girls' and boys' traditional childhood peer relations may foster different norms for the expression of assertion and affiliation in adolescence and adulthood. The emphasis on independence and dominance traditionally seen in boys' peer groups is contrasted with the emphasis on interpersonal closeness and exclusivity traditionally seen in girls' peer groups. Although competition and cooperation are common in both girls' and boys' peer groups, their relative emphases and forms often differ. These patterns may lead to different expectations and skills regarding school achievement and interpersonal intimacy. Furthermore, gender-related differences in social norms may also be associated with communication difficulties and power asymmetries in adolescent and adult male-female relationships. To illustrate, I present new research that finds that young women and men differ in responsiveness and support during intimate conversations with same- or cross-gender friends. I conclude by providing some recommendations for parents and teachers interested in encouraging cross-gender play and gender-role flexibility.

Finally, in Chapter Six, Eleanor Maccoby offers her overview of the ideas raised in the first five chapters. Maccoby's "Gender and Relationships: A Developmental Account" (1990) is a landmark review of the development of gender segregation and its consequences on psychosocial development across the life span. The chapters in this volume provide further elaborations on the themes that Maccoby addressed in her earlier review.

As I have highlighted in these notes, the contributors to this volume have addressed complementary approaches to the study of this topic. Taken together, the reviews and new research presented in these chapters suggest that the development of gender segregation is due to a combination of factors that have differential effects at different ages. The initial emergence of same-gender peer preferences may be due to a combination of differences in behavioral style (Chapters One and Four), emotional arousal (Chapter Two) and cognitive stereotyping (Chapter Three). In contrast, the subsequent maintenance of gender segregation may rely more on cognitive factors (Chapters Three and Five) and social norms (Chapter Five). It also appears that gender segregation may contribute to the development of gender differences in psychological preferences and skills over time. Most notably, this includes differences in academic achievement and intimacy (Chapters Four and Five). In these ways, gender segregation has an important impact on people's lives.

Campbell Leaper
Editor

References

Block, J. H. "Differential Premises Arising from Differential Socialization of the Sexes: Some Conjectures." *Child Development*, 1983, *54*, 1335–1354.

Carter, D. B. "The Roles of Peers in Sex Role Socialization." In D. B. Carter (ed.), *Current Conceptions of Sex Roles and Sex Typing: Theory and Research*. New York: Praeger, 1987.

Cherry-Wilkinson, L., and Marrett, C. B. (eds.). *Gender Influences in Classroom Interaction*. San Diego: Academic Press, 1985.

Goodenough, F. *Developmental Psychology: An Introduction to the Study of Human Behavior*. New York: Appleton-Century, 1934.

Gottman, J. M., and Levenson, R. W. "The Social Psychophysiology of Marriage." In P. Noller and M. A. Fitzpatrick (eds.), *Perspectives on Marital Interaction*. Philadelphia: Multilingual Matters, 1988.

Hare-Mustin, R. T., and Marecek, J. "The Meaning of Difference: Gender Theory, Postmodernism, and Psychology." *American Psychologist*, 1988, *43*, 455–464.

Huston, A. C. "The Development of Sex-Typing: Themes from Recent Research." *Developmental Review*, 1985, *5*, 1–17.

Leaper, C. "Gender Issues in Peer Relations." Panel presentation at the Society for Research in Child Development Pre-Conference on Peer Relations, New Orleans, Mar. 24, 1993.

Liss, M. B. "Learning Gender-Related Skills Through Play." In M. B. Liss (ed.), *Social and Cognitive Skills: Sex Roles and Children's Play*. San Diego: Academic Press, 1983.

Lloyd, B., and Duveen, G. *Gender Identities and Education: The Impact of Starting School*. New York: St. Martin's Press, 1992.

Lockheed, M. E., and Klein, S. S. "Sex Equity in Classroom Organization and Climate." In S. S. Klein (ed.), *Handbook for Achieving Sex Equity Through Education*. Baltimore: Johns Hopkins University Press, 1985.

Maccoby, E. E. "Gender as a Social Category." *Developmental Psychology*, 1988, *24*, 755–765.

Maccoby, E. E. "Gender and Relationships: A Developmental Account." *American Psychologist*, 1990, *45*, 513–520.

Maccoby, E. E., and Jacklin, C. N. "Gender Segregation in Childhood." In E. H. Reese (ed.), *Advances in Child Development and Behavior*. Vol. 20. San Diego: Academic Press, 1987.

Maltz, D. N., and Borker, R. A. "A Cultural Approach to Male-Female Miscommunication." In J. J. Gumperz (ed.), *Language and Social Identity*. New York: Cambridge University Press, 1982.

Parten, M. B. "Social Participation Among Preschool Children." *Journal of Abnormal and Social Psychology*, 1932, *27*, 243–269.

Thorne, B. *Gender Play: Girls and Boys in School*. New Brunswick, N.J.: Rutgers University Press, 1993.

Thorne, B., and Luria, Z. "Sexuality and Gender in Children's Daily Worlds." *Social Problems*, 1986, *33*, 176–190.

Whiting, B. B., and Edwards, C. P. *Children of Different Worlds: The Formation of Social Behavior.* Cambridge, Mass.: Harvard University Press, 1988.

CAMPBELL LEAPER is assistant professor of psychology at the University of California, Santa Cruz.

Contextual and developmental factors that may result in same-sex peer preferences may be observed among two-year-olds prior to the emergence of gender segregation as a dominant pattern in their playgroups.

The Emergence of Gender Segregation in Toddler Playgroups

Lisa A. Serbin, Lora C. Moller, Judith Gulko, Kimberly K. Powlishta, Karen A. Colburne

Gender segregation, the predominance of same-sex groupings, is a pervasive, readily observable characteristic of children's playgroups. Children show non-random patterns of gender association by age three or four, and the phenomenon seems to intensify gradually during early and middle childhood (Hartup, 1983; Lockheed and Klein, 1985; Maccoby and Jacklin, 1987). Over time, the consequences of gender segregation may be extensive. Boys and girls appear to learn and practice different social and cognitive skills within their respective playgroups, with resulting gender differences in patterns of social relations and in academic, recreational, and occupational interests and achievements.

In this chapter, we present the findings from a naturalistic study of five groups of toddlers who had begun attending preschool a few months before the study started. Our purpose was to examine factors that might encourage gender segregation in groups where preferences for same-sex peers were not yet observable or only beginning to appear. To obtain an adequate sampling of behavior across a variety of play situations and social contexts, we videotaped

This research was partially supported by grants from Fonds pour la Formation de Chercheurs et d'Aide à la Recherche (FCAR) of the Ministry of Education of Quebec and the Social Sciences and Humanities Research Council (SSHRC) of Canada. The authors would like to thank the children and staffs of St. Andrew's Nursery School and Rainbow Preschool in Montreal for making this study possible. Correspondence may be addressed to: Lisa A. Serbin, Centre for Research in Human Development and Department of Psychology, Concordia University, 1455 de Maisonneuve Blvd. West, Montreal, Quebec, H3G 1M8, Canada.

the children during free play twice a week, over periods of four to six months. Once we had established that gender segregation was an emerging but not yet dominant pattern, we proceeded to examine various aspects of the children's behavior and classroom functioning that might encourage same-sex association.

Theoretical Perspective

Our hypotheses were primarily based on the theory of behavioral compatibility. Originally suggested in the 1930s (Parten, 1932; Goodenough, 1934), this theory postulates that young children choose play partners whose behavior is compatible with their own. Compatibility might include common interests in specific activities and/or similar or complementary styles of play and social behavior. Thus, if children found same-sex peers' interests and abilities compatible, they would increasingly seek out same-sex playmates. We used this approach to formulate hypotheses regarding behavior in same-sex contexts, to compare the behavior of preferred playmates, and to compare children who showed a preference for same-sex peers with those who did not.

A second conceptual approach that influenced the design of our study was cognitive-developmental theory. Cognitive theorists have suggested that the development of gender identity, the ability to correctly identify the gender of others and of oneself, motivates children to seek out other children perceived as "similar" (that is, of the same gender). Children do this in order to learn more about the behaviors associated with gender roles, and because the children perceived as "like me" are positively valued (see Chapter Three). In this perspective, toddlers who have begun to segregate themselves by gender would be more likely to have developed gender identity, and to know relatively more about sex-role norms, than children who have not yet developed a preference for same-sex peers. Accordingly, we looked to see whether early gender-related knowledge might differentiate children who had developed a preference for same-sex peers from those who had not yet shown a preference.

Group Context Versus Individual Differences

In the last few years, researchers have made a substantial shift in the way they view the psychology of gender differences, moving away from a primary emphasis on individual differences to a recognition of the importance of contextual and group phenomena (Maccoby, 1990). It has been established that gender segregation begins around three years of age, but what remains unclear is whether the emergence of this preference for same-sex playmates is due to the individual characteristics and preferences of certain children, or whether group/contextual phenomena that apply generally to children are more important in both the appearance and maintenance of gender segregation.

We reasoned that both group/contextual and individual factors might influence preschoolers to seek out same-sex playmates. From the contextual perspective, there might be elements of the same-sex situation that would be generally attractive to young children. However, it might also be true that individual children would be attracted to same-sex peers because of personal preferences for particular activities or social interaction styles. Drawing hypotheses from compatibility theory and from a cognitive-developmental perspective, we asked a series of questions about the ways both group contexts and individual factors might foster increasing gender segregation among toddlers.

Method

We used both videotapes and teacher observations to collect data on fifty-seven toddlers.

Subjects. The fifty-seven children (twenty-eight males and twenty-nine females) from middle-class families who participated in the study ranged in age from 26 to 40 months at the start of data collection (mean age = 34.8 months). They were observed during their first year of preschool attendance in one of the five participating classes. The children all spoke English although some were from bilingual homes (English and French or another European or Asian language). There were ten Asian children and two black children in the sample; the remaining children were white. An additional ninety-four older children (ages four and up) from the five classes were available as potential play partners for the focal subjects.

Behavioral Measures. Children were videotaped during free play periods in their classrooms approximately twice a week by one of four female data collectors. Each of the data collectors had participated in a two-week familiarization period, so that the children were accustomed to the presence of the researchers and the hand-held video camera. During data collection, a time-sampling procedure was employed: target children were observed in random order for ten seconds each, with the cycle of observations repeated from three to seven times during each taping session. In three of the classes, observations began in the fall and continued throughout the school year; the other two classes were observed during the second semester only.

An average of seventy-five ten-second intervals (or 12.5 minutes) was recorded for each child. Coders then viewed the videotapes and recorded the children's behavior according to a coding system developed for the study. The major coding categories included group composition (number and sex of children playing with the target child), teacher presence or absence in the group, frequency and type of social behavior (for example, interactive play, parallel play, or watching others), type of toy or ongoing play activity, intensity of play, and activity level. Inter-observer agreement was established at above 80 percent in all categories. The kappa coefficient, which corrects for chance agreement, was .78.

Teacher Ratings and Tests of Gender Knowledge. Teachers were asked to rate each of the children on a twenty-six–item checklist that focused on descriptions of classroom behavior and social interaction styles. In addition, twenty-eight children, drawn from three classes, were given a test of their awareness of gender identity (Leinbach and Fagot, 1986) and their knowledge of the traditional sex-typing of children's activities and adult occupations (Edelbrock and Sugawara, 1978).

Results

Although more research is needed, our results suggest that the emergence of gender segregation is not a consequence of the toddler's desire to act in accordance with his or her perceptions of "proper" gender-role behavior.

Gender Segregation: An Emerging Pattern. As anticipated, we found that the young preschoolers played in mixed-sex more often than same-sex situations. However, rates of play in same-sex dyads, as opposed to larger groups, were more frequent than play in mixed-sex dyads (Gulko and Serbin, under review). Overall, the children spent about half of their play time in mixed-sex groupings and about a quarter of that time in same-sex groupings. About 60 percent of dyadic play was same-sex (thus 40 percent was in mixed-sex groupings), and 22 percent of play in larger groups was same-sex (thus 78 percent was in mixed-sex groups).

Even in larger groups, the proportions of boys and girls were often significantly different from chance proportions. Based on frequency of participation in same- versus mixed-sex groups, and controlling for the number of girls and boys present during observations, 62 percent of the girls and 21 percent of the boys played with same-sex peers at above chance levels. When we observed children's most preferred play partners (that is, "best friends"), there was no significant difference in the number having a same- versus an other-sex child as the most frequent play partner. However, descriptively, 66 percent of the girls and 46 percent of the boys played most often with a peer of the same sex.

From these results, it appeared that gender segregation was beginning to occur, especially in dyadic situations and among the girls, but was still not a dominant pattern. Accordingly, we proceeded with a series of analyses related to the behavioral compatibility hypothesis. We began by exploring whether segregated contexts elicited more socially compatible behavior than did mixed-sex contexts.

Group Context: Comparison of Social Play Patterns. The behavioral compatibility hypothesis suggests that girls seek out girls and boys seek out other boys as playmates because same-sex children may have similar or complementary styles of interaction. However, there are no marked sex differences in social interaction patterns among two- to three-year-olds (see, for example, Eckerman, Whatley, and Kutz, 1975; Holmberg, 1980). However, it may be that children modulate or vary their behavior in different contexts, so that their play is more stimulating when they are with same-sex peers. This might occur for girls and boys generally, meaning that behavior would tend to be different when a child is in a same-sex rather than in a mixed-sex situation, regardless of the child's individual level of social development or style of sociability. If so, children might be increasingly drawn to same-sex situations because they find them interesting, stimulating, and enjoyable.

To see whether the children modulated their behavior across same- and mixed-sex playgroups, we compared each child's behavior in different contexts (Gulko and Serbin, under review), classified by gender composition and by size (dyadic or larger), to determine whether children's play was more socially interactive in same-sex contexts and, conversely, to see whether play in mixed-sex contexts tended to involve more distal forms of social relations, (that is, parallel play and watching rather than interacting). The frequencies of *social interaction* (verbally interacting and making physical contact and/or being involved in common activity with a shared goal), *parallel play* (playing near another child but not interacting), and *watching* (not playing or interacting but focused visually on another child's activities) were compared across same- and mixed-gender dyads and groups, controlling for the number of observations made in each context. The results of these analyses generally supported our prediction that play in same-sex contexts would stimulate more social inter-action, while play in mixed-sex contexts would involve less interaction and more distal peer relations.

In dyadic groupings, more social interaction was observed within same- than mixed-sex pairs. Rates of social interaction in both same- and mixed-sex larger groups were generally lower and not significantly different from each other. In contrast, parallel play and watching, both noninteractive categories, occurred more often when the children were in mixed-sex groupings. Inter-estingly, there were no sex differences in the effects of different contexts on the children's behavior: both girls and boys were more sociable in same- than mixed-sex dyads and engaged in more parallel play and watching when they were with children of the other sex.

Our interpretation of these results is that, even at this early age, children are more likely to engage in interactive play with same-sex children, while they are more apt to watch or play alongside children of the other sex without inter-acting. Assuming that children find interactive play generally more enjoyable and stimulating, we would then expect them to increasingly seek out same-sex peers as play partners. Over time, and with increasing experience in a same-sex context, girls and boys may then develop distinctive social styles and skills (see, for example, Serbin, Sprafkin, Elman, and Doyle, 1982). And it may become increasingly difficult for them to interact compatibly with other-sex children who have developed a different set of skills, styles, and social expec-tations. But we do not know why children modulate their behavior according to the sex of their play partners, and this remains an intriguing topic for future research.

Although our findings apply to the studied children generally and to both sexes, it may be that some children begin to prefer same-sex contexts earlier or more extensively than others. If so, these children will have greater and ear-lier exposure to the experience of the same-sex group and to whatever effects the segregation experience has on social and cognitive development. Accord-ingly, we shifted our perspective to look at individual differences in children's play styles and how young children seek out compatible peers. We then tried to relate individual differences in play styles to gender segregation.

Toddler Preference for Compatible Playmates. The literature on play and friendship in preschoolers suggests that toddlers have distinct and moderately stable preferences for particular play partners in group situations (see, for example, Howes, 1983). As social behavior and play patterns become increasingly sex-typed over the early preschool years, a preference for playing with others who have similar or compatible play styles might gradually result in a preference for same-sex play partners.

As a first step in exploring the role of toddlers' peer preferences in the emergence of gender segregation, we compared the social play patterns of the toddlers in our study with those of their most preferred playmates to see if reliable correlations could be found between the social behaviors of playmates at this age (Moller, 1991). We identified for each child the peer with whom the child was most often observed throughout the study. As indicated earlier, there was no significant tendency for a child to play most often with a same-sex peer. Although nineteen of the girls and thirteen of the boys did have a preferred partner of the same sex, ten girls and fifteen boys were observed most often with a specific peer of the other sex.

Classroom observations and teacher ratings were factor analyzed to produce dimensions of play behavior, and the scores of each target child were correlated with those of her or his most preferred playmate. Significant positive correlations between playmates were found for the observational dimensions of *watching* and *adult-oriented* play. Significant negative correlations indicated that children observed to be highly *social* in their play had play partners who were low on watching and adult-oriented play. Children with high scores on the dimension of *vigor,* which reflected generally high levels of physical energy and activity, had playmates with low scores on *intensity,* a dimension that involved a more focused, concentrated style of play. In other words, children who tended to engage in highly vigorous play avoided children with a more focused, less active style. These correlations indicated that children tended to select playmates whose play styles both resembled and complemented their own.

However, because the observations from which these descriptive factors were derived were at least partially performed while the target children and their playmates were interacting, each child may have been directly influenced by the peer's behavior. This could artificially inflate the correlations between play partners' behavioral styles. However, correlations based on teacher ratings do not have this potentially confounding circumstance, since the teachers completed the forms for each child independently, and when we compared play partners' behavior based on teacher ratings, we found a similar pattern of correspondence between target children's and preferred playmates' play styles. After factor analyzing the teacher rating scales and extracting dimensions of social behavior, we found that the children rated as *socially sensitive* by their teachers had playmates also rated as socially sensitive. Children with play styles viewed as *disruptive* had play partners rated low on *popularity* with peers, while the popular children selected playmates rated high on social sensitivity. These findings again support the hypothesis that play styles systematically affect playmate choices, with toddlers selecting playmates with similar and complementary play styles.

Over time, if play styles of boys and girls become increasingly distinctive, same-sex preferences would emerge from this preference for compatible partners. Accordingly, our final set of analyses focused on children who had begun to prefer same-sex contexts, to see whether segregating children (those preferring same-sex play partners) had distinctive characteristics when compared with the children who showed no preference.

Comparison of Segregating and Nonsegregating Children

Gender differences in activity preferences and social behavior begin to appear during children's second year and become increasingly marked and consistent during the preschool period. As gender differences develop, children's preference for compatible playmates might lead those children who have developed sex-typed interests and social behavioral styles to interact with similarly sex-typed children. Hence, among a group of toddlers, the segregating children would be drawn together by a common interest in the same sex-typed play materials or activities and/or because they enjoy playing with peers who have similar behavioral styles and repertoires. If this hypothesis was correct, we could expect children who had begun segregating to show more sex-typed preferences for play activities than nonsegregating children. Similarly, we could expect segregating children to demonstrate more sex-typed patterns of social behavior.

Alternatively, it has been suggested that children may seek out same-sex peers as a result of cognitive-developmental phenomena (see Chapter Three). When a child acquires categories corresponding to gender and begins to accurately label herself or himself as female or male, that child is motivated to learn more about her or his gender role by seeking out peers perceived as similar. The child also finds peers she or he perceives as similar to be attractive and likeable. Hence children who have acquired a stable *gender identity* and have learned relatively more than other children about other gender-related concepts (such as sex roles) might be more likely to demonstrate gender preferences in their playmate choices.

In our sample, 42 percent of the children (21 percent of the boys and 62 percent of the girls) played with same-sex children at above chance levels over the course of the observations (Moller and Serbin, under review). These two groups, segregating girls and segregating boys, were compared with the remaining girls and boys in an Analysis of Variance design, including sex of child and peer preference (segregating or nonsegregating) as predictors. The first two dependent measures in these analyses were rates of play with "masculine" and "feminine" toys in the classroom. The scales for determining which toys were used more often by boys and which by girls were developed and measured empirically, based on classroom observations, using a procedure developed by Connor and Serbin (1977). Each child then received a score reflecting how often he or she used the toys in each scale relative to other same-sex children. A second set of dependent measures was derived from factor analysis of the teacher rating scales. These scales showed overall sex differences: *active/disruptive* behavior (boys higher than girls) and *socially sensitive* behavior (girls higher than boys).

For these two sets of variables, we expected interactions between sex of child and peer preferences, with the segregating children showing traditionally sex-typed patterns (for example, segregating boys would be high on play with masculine toys and disruption and segregating girls low, but a converse pattern would hold for play with feminine toys and social sensitivity), while nonsegregating children of each sex would be more similar to each other and generally intermediate on these variables.

For the sex-typed toy scales variables, we did not find any significant interactions. That is, segregating children did not show more sex-typed toy and activity preferences than did nonsegregating children. This confirms previous research that has found that the frequency of play with sex-stereotyped toys and activities was not related to a child's preference for same-sex playmates (Maccoby and Jacklin, 1987). The social/behavioral factors, however, did show the expected pattern. The segregating boys were perceived by teachers as the most active/disruptive, although boys and segregating children of both sexes in general were seen as more active/disruptive than nonsegregating girls. On the social sensitivity scoring, the interaction of sex and peer preference was significant, with segregating girls rated higher than segregating boys, and nonsegregating girls and boys being intermediate.

These findings appear to complement the preliminary results described in Chapter Two of this volume, addressing the relation between teachers' ratings of children's positive and negative social behaviors and their tendencies to play in segregated or nonsegregated groups.

Gender Awareness and Sex-Role Knowledge

Our last hypothesis, derived from cognitive-developmental theory, led us to predict that segregating children would be more aware of gender identity and of sex roles than nonsegregating children. Virtually all the children were able to correctly identify their own and others' gender. For this reason, gender identity was obviously not a useful variable on which to compare the groups. On the test of sex-role knowledge (in which the children were asked to identify which child, a boy or a girl, was most likely to play with a series of toys), there was a wide range of scores. Comparing segregating with nonsegregating children on this measure of sex-role knowledge did not, however, differentiate the groups. In other words, segregating children did not show more knowledge of sex roles, at least regarding the stereotyping of toys and activities, than did nonsegregating children. Hence, there was no support for the idea that segregation might be a consequence of sex-role awareness.

Conclusion

Our study clarifies a number of issues but also raises or leaves unsolved a number of other issues. A child's play with another toddler of the same sex seems to facilitate social interaction, while play with one or more children of the other sex leads to more passive social relations. This would seem to encourage more same-sex play. However, we do not know why children at this age behave more sociably with a same-sex peer. This will be an important issue for further research. We also know that toddlers and their preferred playmates behave similarly. Is this because toddlers seek out compatible friends or, possibly, because they adopt the styles of their playmates? Of course, it is possible that children seek out compatible playmates and also become increasingly similar in behavioral style to their play partners as they play together over time.

Our study also shows that segregating toddlers are more behaviorally sex-typed: the boys more active and disruptive, the girls more socially sensitive, than children who have not developed a preference for same-sex peers. However, is it a preference for compatible (behaviorally sex-typed) friends that draws the segregating children together, or is it experience in the same-sex group that gradually makes these children's behavior more sex-typed? We suspect that both may be true. Longitudinal or experimental designs will be needed to clarify these issues.

Finally, we have demonstrated that preferences for sex-typed toys do not seem to be an important factor influencing gender segregation at this age: peer preferences are more related to social style and compatibility. Similarly, cognitive-developmental factors, specifically gender identity and knowledge of sex roles, do not seem to discriminate segregating from nonsegregating toddlers. It is possible, however, that these variables may be related to gender segregation at later stages of development (see Chapters Three, Four, and Five).

We conclude that gender segregation must be examined from diverse theoretical and methodological perspectives to be understood. A developmental perspective is also necessary, because the phenomenon seems to change and to be influenced by different factors at different stages. Finally, the cumulative consequences of gender segregation and its developmental and possible limiting effects must be taken into account as it becomes an increasingly dominant pattern across middle childhood, persisting, in different forms, into adolescence and adulthood.

It is also important to remember, however, that while virtually all children are exposed to the same-sex context and its consequences, individual children will place different limits on the extent to which they play with same-sex peers. Stable individual differences in degree of same-sex peer preference are found for children in middle childhood (Serbin, Powlishta, and Gulko, 1993) and are related to flexible sex-role attitudes and to egalitarian patterns of child rearing at home. These individual differences deserve further study. For example, it would be interesting to know whether children whose peer interaction patterns are less segregated develop a broader range of skills and interests in comparison with children who have more exclusive patterns of same-sex association.

Gender segregation, of course, does not have to mean that only sex-typed activities or skills are practiced within the single-sex context. It is possible to create a single-sex environment in which skills that are not sex-typed, or that are stereotyped as appropriate for the other sex, are also learned. Conversely, we cannot assume children in a coeducational context will practice patterns of behavior that are not traditionally sex-typed. In some circumstances, mixed-sex situations may foster more sex-typed behavior than single-sex situations. Similar thinking has influenced the ongoing interest in utilizing the apparent social effects of same-sex contexts to enhance learning and to foster the development of such positive characteristics as self-esteem. Historically, however, single-sex groupings have often been used to provide to one gender experiences and opportunities that have not been made available to the other, and there is a vast difference between spontaneous gender segregation, in which children primarily interact with peers of their own sex but can move back and forth within different peer groupings, and enforced segregation in which one group has no opportunity to interact or to benefit from what the other group learns.

While children like to play with children they perceive as similar to themselves, the dimensions on which they define themselves and others as similar may be heavily influenced by socialization and context. Gender, race, and ethnicity do not have to be primary or necessary dimensions for association; alternatives may be common interests, skills, or compatible behavioral styles. The "ethic" promoted by the organizers of a particular situation probably plays a major role in determining the salience of specific social dimensions within that situation and how much social interaction occurs between same- and other-sex children and whether the children's behavior is traditionally sex-typed. Moreover, given the reality of mixed-sex workplaces and homes, it may be essential that males and females learn to work and play together in mixed-gender situations if egalitarian work and social relationships are to develop. Young children are typically interested and eager to play with others with whom they can interact in a mutually compatible and enjoyable way. While playgroups may "naturally" become increasingly segregated as the children develop, this phenomenon is not exclusive. It may be worthwhile, considering the long-term consequences, to structure play and learning situations to allow egalitarian, cross-gender interactions to continue and flourish alongside same-gender relationships during early and middle childhood.

References

Connor, J. M., and Serbin, L. A. "Behaviorally Based Masculine- and Feminine-Activity Preference Scales for Preschoolers: Correlates with Other Classroom Behaviors and Cognitive Tests." *Child Development,* 1977, *48,* 1411–1416.

Eckerman, C., Whatley, J. L., and Kutz, S. "Growth of Social Play with Peers During the Second Year of Life." *Developmental Psychology,* 1975, *11,* 42–49.

Edelbrock, C., and Sugawara, A. I. "Acquisition of Sex-Typed Preferences in Preschool-Aged Children." *Developmental Psychology, 1978, 14,* 614–623.

Goodenough, F. *Developmental Psychology: An Introduction to the Study of Human Behavior.* New York: Appleton-Century, 1934.

Gulko, J., and Serbin, L. A. "Sociability in Same- and Mixed-Sex Toddler Groups: An Antecedent of Gender Segregation?" Under review.

Hartup, W. W. "Peer Relations." In P. H. Mussen (ed.), *Handbook of Child Psychology.* (4th ed.) Vol. 4: *Socialization, Personality, and Social Development.* (E. M. Hetherington, vol. ed.) New York: Wiley, 1983.

Holmberg, M. C. "The Development of Social Interchange Patterns from 12 to 42 Months." *Child Development, 1980, 51,* 448–456.

Howes, C. "Patterns of Friendship." *Child Development, 1983, 54,* 1044–1053.

Huston, A. C. "Sex-Typing." In P. H. Mussen (ed.), *Handbook of Child Psychology.* (4th ed.) Vol. 4: *Socialization, Personality, and Social Development.* (E. M. Hetherington, vol. ed.) New York: Wiley, 1983.

Leinbach, M. D., and Fagot, B. I. "Acquisition of Gender Labels: A Test for Toddlers." *Sex Roles,* 1986, *15,* 655–666.

Lockheed, M., and Klein, S. "Sex Equity in Classroom Organization and Climate." In S. Klein (ed.), *Handbook for Achieving Sex Equity Through Education.* Baltimore: Johns Hopkins University Press, 1985.

Maccoby, E. E. "Gender and Relationships: A Developmental Account." *American Psychologist,* 1990, *45* (4), 513–520.

Maccoby, E. E., and Jacklin, C. N. "Gender Segregation in Childhood." In H. Reese (ed.), *Advances in Child Development and Behavior.* Vol. 20. San Diego: Academic Press, 1987.

Moller, L. C. "Toddler Peer Preferences: The Role of Gender Awareness, Sex-Typed Toy Preferences and Compatible Play Styles." Unpublished doctoral dissertation, Concordia University, Montreal, 1991.

Moller, L. C., and Serbin, L. A. "Antecedents to Toddler Gender Segregation: Cognitive Consonance, Sex-Typed Toy Preferences and Behavioral Compatibility." Under review.

Parten, M. B. "Social Participation Among Preschool Children." *Journal of Abnormal and Social Psychology,* 1932, *27,* 243–269.

Serbin, L. A., Powlishta, K. K., and Gulko, J. "The Development of Sex Typing in Middle Childhood." *Monographs of the Society for Research in Child Development,* 1993, *58* (2, Serial 232).

Serbin, L. A., Sprafkin, C., Elman, M., and Doyle, A. B. "The Early Development of Sex-Differentiated Patterns of Social Influence." *Canadian Journal of Behavioral Science,* 1982, *14* (4), 350–363.

LISA A. SERBIN *is professor of psychology at Concordia University in Montreal.*

LORA C. MOLLER *is assistant professor of psychology at Concordia University.*

JUDITH GULKO *is an associate faculty member at Miracosta College and is in private practice in Encinitas, California.*

KIMBERLY K. POWLISHTA *is assistant professor of psychology at Northern Illinois University.*

KAREN A. COLBURNE *is a graduate student in psychology at Concordia University.*

Boys and girls may differ in their physiological responses to social interactions and these differences may set the stage for gender segregation.

Physiological, Emotional, and Behavioral Correlates of Gender Segregation

Richard A. Fabes

The fact that children play primarily in same-sex peer groups is well documented but not well understood (Maccoby, 1990; Maccoby and Jacklin, 1987). Gender segregation is an almost universal phenomenon, found in all cultural settings in which children are in social groups that permit choice. The data presented in this volume provide consistent and reliable evidence that boys and girls prefer to play with children of their own sex, although the degree to which gender segregation occurs depends on contextual factors (see also Thorne, 1986).

Although several hypotheses have been put forward to explain gender segregation, Maccoby (for example, 1990) has suggested that two factors play a particularly important role. First, she suggests that girls find it difficult to influence boys, and thus, girls find it aversive to interact with boys because boys are unresponsive to girls' influence attempts. As a result, girls begin to avoid interaction with boys. Second, she proposes that the rough-and-tumble play style of boys and boys' orientation towards dominance and competition are avoided by girls. These aspects of boys' interactions appear to be aversive to most girls because these aspects are highly physical. In turn, boys appear to find playing with girls less interesting than playing with other boys because

The research reported in this chapter was supported in part by a grant from the National Science Foundation (BNS-8807784) to Richard Fabes and Nancy Eisenberg, and by an Arizona State University Arts, Sciences, and Humanities Faculty Research grant (RWR-C311) awarded to Richard Fabes. Appreciation is expressed to Nancy Eisenberg for her helpful comments on an earlier version of the manuscript.

girls do not respond to boys' rough-and-tumble, hierarchically dominant styles of play.

The purpose of this chapter is to review existing evidence and to present new evidence that supports the contention that the differences among boys and girls in influenceability and dominating behavior may be due in part to gender differences in physiological arousal and regulation. Building on a model proposed by Gottman and Levenson (1988), I will argue these differences mediate or moderate early patterns of gender segregation and present new empirical data that examine the relation between children's arousability and their peer preferences. More specifically, the model presented in this chapter is based on the idea that the thresholds for arousal differ for boys and girls, and that boys have more difficulty than girls in regulating their arousal once they are aroused. Moreover, the model proposes that the conditions and contexts that boys and girls find physiologically arousing are different. Finally, I discuss the implications of these findings for future research and conceptualization.

Arousal, Regulation, and Social Behavior

Several researchers have reported sex differences in the physiological reactions of children and adults (see Hoyenga and Hoyenga, 1979), some beginning very early in development. For example, Davis (1991) found that newborn boys exhibited greater behavioral reactivity and adrenocortical responses to some forms of stress at birth than did newborn girls. Because of the age of the children in her study (twenty-four to sixty hours old), Davis concluded that gender differences in physiological and behavioral reactivity exist before extensive socialization has occurred and that the greater reactivity in males may have a biological basis.

Other researchers have noted that male infants evidence greater physiological reactivity than do female infants. Moss (1974) reported a tendency for male infants to show greater irritability and greater difficulty in regulating their equilibrium, being generally fussier and more difficult to calm than female infants. In contrast to males, female infants were found to evidence shorter protest episodes, to which the mother was less likely to respond. Female infants tended to restore themselves to a state of equilibrium without maternal intervention more often than did male infants. Haviland and Malatesta (1981) reviewed more recent evidence and also concluded that male infants are more irritable and less soothable than female infants. According to Haviland and Malatesta, females are physiologically more capable of tolerating emotional arousal and can do so for longer periods of time before becoming dysregulated and distressed.

Although these studies provide some support for an overall sex difference in infant arousability, their findings remain controversial because researchers have failed to consider differences in the early experiential histories of boys and girls (for example, the circumcision of male newborns). More recent assessments of young infants' difficultness have failed to find significant sex differences (Marcus, Maccoby, Jacklin, and Doering, 1985).

In adults, there is more consistent evidence that males appear to be more adversely affected by stress and have a more difficult time recouping from stress-induced arousal states than females (Gray, 1971). For example, although cortisol (a hormone released by stress) is normatively higher in females than males, males have been found to take longer than females to return to baseline levels once cortisol levels have risen (Erskine, Stern, and Levine, 1975). Frankenhaeuser and colleagues (Frankenhaeuser, 1982; Rauste-von Wright, von Wright, and Frankenhaeuser, 1981) found that under stressful and demanding conditions (that is, test taking) both young men and women showed increases in adrenaline production relative to individuals in a control (nonstressful) condition. However, the increase for males was greater than the increase for females, and only males showed a significant increase in cortisol production (Frankenhaeuser and others, 1978).

Thus, although the work of Frankenhaeuser and colleagues has established the existence of sex differences in adults' and adolescents' physiological responses to stress, these differences have not consistently been established in childhood. In some new data from our lab, Nancy Eisenberg and I have some evidence documenting similar differences in children's responses. As depicted in Figure 2.1, differences in preschool boys' and girls' responses were found to occur as a function of whether they were taken during a calm, baseline condition (watching a relaxing film about dolphins swimming in the sea) or during exposure to an emotionally evocative stimulus (watching a film about a child who was burned and then teased about her scars). Specifically, in the evocative context, boys' skin conductance responses peaked more quickly and took longer to return to baseline levels than did girls': $p < .05$. However, there were no differences in any skin conductance index taken under baseline conditions. Moreover, girls tended to manifest more intense skin responses to the baseline context whereas boys tended to manifest more intense responses to the evocative context (although these differences were not significant).

Thus, there is some evidence that sex differences in boys' and girls' patterns of physiological responding differ only under evocative conditions. Moreover, the pattern suggests that under evocative conditions, boys tend to peak in arousal more quickly and return to baseline more slowly than girls. The question then becomes how these differences in physiological response and in the eliciting contexts contribute to gender segregation.

Recently, Eisenberg and I have begun to explore how children's emotional arousal is related to their social behaviors and to others' perceptions of the children (Eisenberg and Fabes, 1992). Specifically, we have argued that individuals who are unable to maintain their emotional arousal within tolerable levels (that is, who become overaroused) are expected to behave in ways that may not facilitate positive interactions in evocative and arousing social situations, and we have identified two individual difference variables that we believe influ-

Figure 2.1. Mean Skin Conductance Responses by Sex and Context

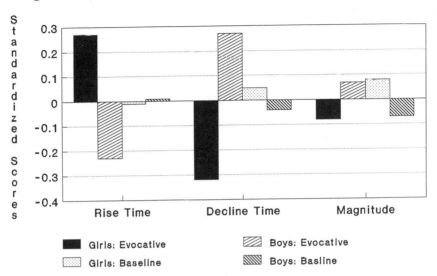

ence the degree to which individuals become emotionally aroused in social contexts (Eisenberg and Fabes, 1992). These two variables include, first, an individual's dispositional level of emotional responsivity, particularly the intensity and threshold of responding, and second, an individual's ability to regulate his or her emotional reactions and cope with evocative social contexts. Socially competent behavior is thought to be most likely to occur when individuals are moderately emotionally responsive and optimally regulated. For example, in recent work (Eisenberg and others, in press) we have found that children's emotional arousal and regulatory tendencies predicted social skills for both boys and girls. Specifically, teachers' ratings of children's emotional intensity and problematic coping behaviors (for example, aggressive versus avoidant coping responses) were both inversely related to boys' and girls' social skills.

We believe that emotional intensity (EI) reflects both the intensity and threshold of emotional arousability. Thus, individuals high in EI tend to be more reactive to emotional stimuli than those low in EI (Larsen, Diener, and Emmons, 1986). Is there evidence that boys and girls differ in EI? In a study of preschoolers' emotionality (Eisenberg and others, 1994), we found that teachers rated boys as significantly higher in EI than girls; however, mothers' EI ratings of boys and girls did not vary. Additionally, boys were observed to respond to conflict between peers with more intense anger than were girls. One explanation for these findings is that boys may be particularly more likely

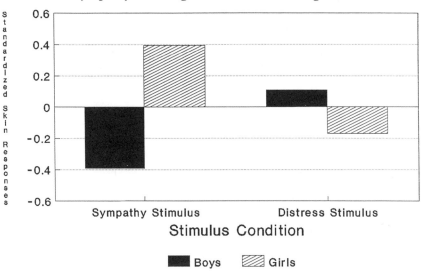

Figure 2.2. Children's Skin Conductance Responses to
Sympathy-Inducing and Distress-Inducing Stimuli

Note: Skin responses for the two studies were computed somewhat differently. See figure sources for precise computation procedures.

Sources: Eisenberg and others, 1991a; Fabes and others, 1994.

to respond with increased arousal and intensity within the context of peer social interaction (as indicated by teachers' and observers' ratings). However, outside of peer interactions, boys and girls may not differ in EI (as indicated by mothers' ratings).

Other studies also reveal evidence that differences in boys' and girls' emotional arousal varies as a function of the context. For example, when children were exposed to a relatively less evocative, sympathy-inducing film, in which a handicapped child talked in a positive tone about her handicap (Eisenberg and others, 1991a), girls evidenced greater arousal (as measured by skin conductance responses) than did boys (see Figure 2.2). In contrast, when other children were exposed to a relatively more evocative, distress-inducing film, in which children were scared about being alone in the house and seeing a stranger lurking outside (Fabes and others, 1994),[1] boys evidenced significantly greater skin conductance arousal than did girls (see Figure 2.2). Thus, boys and girls appear to respond differently to emotionally evocative stimuli, and the contexts that elicit emotional arousal in boys and girls appear to differ.

Emotion regulation, the second individual difference variable of interest, has been viewed in at least two different (but interrelated) ways. First, it has been viewed by persons studying temperament as involving the control of impinging stimuli and internal states, that is, using attentional, activational, or inhibitory mechanisms (Rothbart and Derryberry, 1981). For example, individuals who can regulate their emotional reactivity through allocating attention (shifting their attention away from distressing stimuli) have been found to react more positively to stressful events (Rothbart, Ziaie, and O'Boyle, 1992; Fabes, Eisenberg, and Eisenbud, 1993). Second, emotion regulation also has been viewed as changing cognitive and behavioral efforts to manage specific external or internal demands that are appraised as taxing or exceeding the resources of the individual, that is, coping (Lazarus and Folkman, 1984). Two general modes of coping have been identified: *problem-focused coping* is defined as an effort to modify the source of the problem and *emotion-focused coping* is defined as an effort to reduce emotional distress. Individuals who can regulate their emotional arousal are likely to cope in relatively constructive and controlled ways; indeed, Lazarus and Folkman argue that, in many situations, people first need to regulate negative emotions if they are to facilitate effective problem-solving coping strategies.

Given the different ways that emotion regulation has been viewed, the logical question to ask in regard to the focus of this chapter is, Do boys' and girls' regulate emotional arousal differently? Some evidence for such differences has been found. For example, Miller, Danaher, and Forbes (1986) found that boys' responses to interpersonal stress (for example, conflicts) were more heavy-handed and appeared to be more concerned with the boys' own agenda than were girls' responses, whereas girls were more concerned with maintaining interpersonal harmony. Similarly, Fabes and Eisenberg (1992) found that boys were more likely to vent or use revenge when involved in interpersonal conflict, whereas girls were more likely to actively defend themselves. Boys also have been found to be less likely than girls to seek assistance from others and to utilize problem-solving strategies when stressed (Brodzinsky and others, 1992). Additionally, males frequently score lower than females in measures of regulation, delay of gratification, and impulse control (Block and Block, 1980; Pulkkinen, 1982). Finally, boys appear to be higher on ego defenses that externalize (for example, projection and aggressive-outward defense), and girls may be higher on defense mechanisms that internalize (Cramer, 1979; Nolen-Hoeksema, 1991). All these findings suggest differences in males' and females' styles of regulating emotion. Females appear to be more likely to employ coping and regulatory responses that reflect greater sensitivity to, and use of, their environment; whereas boys' coping responses have been found to be more avoidant, forceful, and uncontrolled.

Although these data suggest an overall gender difference in boys' and girls' abilities to tolerate and cope with arousal states, caution must be used in drawing broad conclusions. As noted by Zaslow and Hayes (1986), there are several possible explanations for these differences. Of particular interest is the possibility that the contexts in which these gender differences have been found (interpersonal conflict, family discord, and so forth) have greater potential for evoking strong emotional arousal in boys than in girls. Moreover, it is possible that the contexts examined contain features particularly likely to trigger problematic responses in boys (for example, in response to hostile or agonistic interactions). It is possible that other contexts may be more likely to arouse girls than boys (see Figure 2.2).

An example of the importance of context appears in a study by Gunnar-Gnechten (1978) that found that boys who could not control a potentially frightening, noxious, noisy toy became more distressed when exposed to it than did boys who had been taught to operate it and, thus, were able to control its onset. Importantly, this relationship between distress and the inability to control the noxious toy was found *only* for boys; ability to control the toy was unrelated to distress for girls. Thus, it appears that certain contextual features are likely to induce differential arousal states, and evoke different responses, in boys and girls. Upon this premise, I have hypothesized a role for arousal in children's gender-segregated play.

Sex Differences in Arousability and Regulation

Basing my view on the evidence presented here, I propose that gender segregation may be due, in part, to differences in boys' and girls' arousal-related responses and how these responses are perceived by others. Specifically, I propose that boys and girls are differentially responsive to different evocative contexts and that these differences may help explain why girls find it difficult to influence boys. Serbin, Sprafkin, Elman, and Doyle (1982) found that young girls' influence attempts were increasingly likely to take the form of polite suggestions as the girls grew older. In contrast, boys' influence attempts more often took the form of direct demands. Serbin, Sprafkin, Elman, and Doyle (1982) also reported that, with age, boys were increasingly less responsive to the style of influence adopted by girls. Similarly, Fagot (1985) reported that boys' behaviors did not appear to be affected by a female's response, but boys did modify their behavior in response to another boy's reaction.

Maccoby (1990) examined several possible explanations of why boys are not influenced by girls and concluded that "we simply do not know why girls' influence styles are ineffective with boys" (p. 515). However, one reason that boys are unresponsive to girls' influence attempts may be that boys' and girls' emotional and behavioral thresholds differ. Recall the data presented earlier regarding differences in boys' and girls' responses to sympathy- versus distress-inducing stimuli. Girls tended to be more physiologically responsive to relatively less evocative, sympathy-inducing stimuli than were boys, whereas boys were found to be more physiologically responsive to relatively more evocative, distress-inducing stimuli.

Thus, it appears that it takes a considerably more power-assertive and arousing style of interaction to influence boys and get them to respond than to influence girls. For example, Maltz and Borker (1982) reported that boys were more likely to use threats, interruptions, and teasing than were girls, whereas girls were more likely than boys to express agreement or acknowledge another's point. Similarly, Leaper (1991) found that boys' verbal exchanges were more controlling and domineering, whereas girls' verbal exchanges involved more positive reciprocity and collaboration, especially with increasing age. Thus, girls' influence attempts may not be evocative enough to elicit desired responses in boys although they are effective with other girls and well adapted to interactions with adults. The difference may be due not only to a lower threshold for evoking optimal arousal in girls but also to increased regulation of girls' arousal once it is raised.

Gender differences in emotional arousability and regulation may also be involved in boys' rough-and-tumble, dominance-oriented play. *Rough-and-tumble play* designates a set of play behaviors that mimic aggressive actions and include a strong arousal component. DiPietro (1981) reports that boys engaged in more rough-and-tumble play than did girls. Whiting and Edwards (1988) found this gender difference in rough-and-tumble play to be true across a variety of cultures. Moreover, this increased rate of rough-and-tumble play in males has been demonstrated in nonhuman species (Suomi, 1977). Thus, within similar environmental situations, boys and girls appeared to react with qualitatively different patterns of play and social interaction. Male-male interactions were characterized more often by aroused physical contact with one another and with stimulus toys. Girls more often attempted to structure the play sessions through rules and suggestions, and contact tended to be verbal and not physical (DiPietro, 1981).

To date, however, the roles that emotional arousability and regulation play in boys' more forceful and domineering play styles have not been directly examined. It is suggested that boys may be particularly sensitive to becoming aroused within the context of evocative social interactions. For example, males appear to respond with aroused interest and a matching response when another male makes a bid to initiate rough play, whereas females withdraw (Meany, Stewart, and Beatty, 1985). Boys appear to find this type of interaction more pleasing and exciting than girls do. Although some investigators have reported that individual differences in aggressiveness or agonistic dominance do not predict rough-and-tumble play (Blurton-Jones, 1972), the highly aroused state involved in such play increases the chance for injuries and mishaps that can easily escalate to angry physical interactions (DiPietro, 1981). Given that boys may have difficulty regulating this arousal, rough-and-tumble play may move quickly into overly exuberant, forceful interactions (including aggression). Although same-sex partners seem to have little difficulty discriminating rough-and-tumble play from aggression, other-sex peers and adults may misinterpret the these interactions, attending to the behavior rather than its context. Indeed, it is often difficult to train research assistants to distinguish rough-and-tumble play from aggression. Thus, the increased arousal-based rough-and-tumble play of boys may have repercussions for how peers are perceived and for the formation of dominance hierarchies (Bukowski, Gauze,

Hoza, and Newcomb, 1993). Additionally, dominant and forceful interactions function to restrict and control social interaction (Savin-Williams, 1979). Boys may find such dominant interactions to be effective ways of regulating social interactions that are potentially overarousing and aversive.

Arousability and Gender Segregation

Although the findings reviewed here are suggestive of a relation between children's arousability and the formation of peer preferences and play behaviors, they remain highly speculative and indirect. Recently, however, Carol Martin, Nancy Eisenberg, and I collected new data that address the relation more directly. These data are from our ongoing longitudinal study of preschoolers' social development and were obtained from ninety children (forty-five boys and forty-five girls; mean age = 57.8 months; SD = 10.13; range = 39 to 79 months). We collected data through several measures.

Index of Arousability. First, to obtain a measure of the children's arousability, we asked their teachers to rate the children's arousal-related responses. The items included on the index were taken from the Emotionality, Activity, Sociability, and Impulsivity (EASI) temperament measure (Buss and Plomin, 1984) and included ratings of each child's emotional threshold (eight items, including, for example, "this child is easily angered," and, "this child get easily upset"; alpha = .92), impulsivity (four items, including, for example, "this child can't stand waiting"; alpha = .79), and activity level (eight items, including, for example, "this child does things vigorously," and, "this child tends to keep busy all the time"; alpha = .82). For each item, the child's primary teacher rated him or her on a scale from 1 (not at all descriptive) to 7 (very descriptive). Thus, higher scores reflect greater levels of the characteristics. A composite *index of arousability* was created by taking the mean across all the items.

Playgroup Observations. For sixty of the children, we also obtained observations of their naturally occurring free play interactions over three months. A scan sampling procedure was utilized, in which observers proceeded through a randomly ordered list of names, focusing briefly (ten seconds) on each subject and immediately coding his or her behavior. For the present purposes, the data of interest were obtained when the target child was interacting with another child. When this occurred, the observer noted the sex of the child or children played with. Subsequently, we coded whether the child was playing with same-sex, other-sex, or mixed-sex peers. To determine reliability, observers conducted simultaneous observations with a trained reliability observer (ten samplings were obtained from each observer). Agreement across all observers ranged from 88 to 100 percent.

Ratings of Positive and Negative Social Behaviors. These ratings were obtained from the children's secondary teacher (the classroom assistant), thus minimizing response bias by obtaining the ratings of children's arousability and social behaviors from different sources. The secondary teachers were asked to rate each child (using the same 1 to 7 scale as before) on three positive social characteristics (helpfulness, sympathy, and kindness) and two negative social characteristics (hostility and greediness). These social behavior items were taken from the Bem Sex-Role Inventory (Bem, 1981). Alphas for the positive and negative social characteristics scales were .83 and .51, respectively.

Sociometric Ratings. A procedure similar to that developed by Asher, Singleton, Tinsley, and Hymel (1979) was used to assess children for same- and other-sex peer preferences. Each child was shown randomly arranged photographs of his or her classmates (one at a time) and asked to indicate how much she or he liked each child. Children indicated their responses using a 3-point picture scale in which a large smile face indicated that the child in the photograph was "really liked a lot" (rating of 3), a small smile face indicated the child was "kind of liked" (rating of 2), and a frown face indicated that the child was not liked (rating of 1). Mean ratings given to same- and other-sex children were then computed (with higher scores reflecting greater liking).

Results. Our data tended to support our hypotheses.

Descriptive Data. Table 2.1 presents the means of the study indexes. They reveal the classic pattern of same-sex peer interactions for both boys and girls and are comparable to findings reported by others (Maccoby and Jacklin, 1987). Boys and girls did not differ in the proportion of play interactions involving same-, other-, and mixed-sex groups. Moreover, teachers did not differ in their ratings of boys' and girls' arousability, positive, or negative social behaviors ($M = 5.39, 5.17$, and 3.07 for boys and $5.33, 5.26$, and 2.83 for girls, respectively). The index of arousability was inversely related to the index of positive social behavior only for boys (all correlations presented are partial correlations, controlling for age): $r(n = 42) = -.31, p < .05$. Additionally, arousability was positively correlated with the index of negative social behavior for both boys and girls: $r(n = 42) = .45, p < .001; r(n = 41) = .40, p < .005$. Thus, arousable boys and girls were rated higher in negative behaviors, and arousable boys also were rated lower in positive social behaviors.

Arousability and Playgroup Preferences. The relation of arousability to playgroup preferences was examined using correlations. A composite index of same-sex play preference was derived by subtracting the proportion of other-sex play from the proportion of same-sex play (Maccoby and Jacklin, 1987). As can be seen in Table 2.2, the composite index of arousability was found to be related to boys' but not girls' playgroup preferences. Specifically, boys who were rated by teachers as being more arousable evidenced greater same-sex preferences and were less likely to play in mixed-sex groups than were boys who were less arousable.

Social Behavior and Playgroup Preferences. Our next set of correlations addressed the relation between teachers' ratings of children's positive and negative social behaviors and the children's tendencies to play with same-, other-, and mixed-sex peers. For both boys and girls, the index of positive social behaviors did relate to peer-group play preferences. Boys who were rated by teachers as being relatively high in the positive social behaviors were relatively

Table 2.1. Mean Proportion of Observed Interactions in Same-Sex, Other-Sex, and Mixed-Sex Playgroups

Playgroup	Mean	Standard Deviation	Minimum	Maximum
Boys (n = 30)				
Same-sex	.62	.11	.31	.80
Other-sex	.14	.07	.03	.31
Mixed-sex	.24	.07	.11	.39
Girls (n = 30)				
Same-sex	.65	.09	.43	.82
Other-sex	.09	.05	.03	.25
Mixed-sex	.26	.07	.15	.39

Table 2.2. Partial Relations (Controlling for Age) of Rated Arousability and Social Behaviors to Observed Playgroup Preferences

Peer-Group Play	Ratings		
	Arousability	Positive Behaviors	Negative Behaviors
Boys			
Same-sex preference	.33*	-.67****	.32*
Mixed-sex preference	-.43**	.51***	-.22
Girls			
Same-sex preference	.13	.38*	.10
Mixed-sex preference	-.12	-.21	-.13

Note: df = 26 for both boys and girls. The index of same-sex preference was computed by subtracting the proportion of opposite-sex play from the proportion of same-sex play.
*$p < .05$.
**$p < .01$.
***$p < .005$.
****$p < .001$.

unlikely to play with other boys and relatively likely to play in mixed-sex groups. Girls who were rated by teachers as higher in the positive social behaviors were relatively likely to play with other girls than with boys. The only significant relation in the ratings of negative social behaviors was found for boys who were rated high in negative social behaviors. These boys were relatively likely to be observed playing with other boys rather than with girls (see Table 2.2).

Sociometric Judgments and Arousability. We also examined the degree to which children's judgments about same- and other-sex children were related to the target child's perceived arousability. When the relations between children's arousability and their sociometric ratings of same- and other-sex children were computed, only the relations for girls were found to be significant. Specifically, girls' sociometric ratings of both same- and other-sex children were inversely related to the girls' arousability: $r(n = 41) = -.33$ and $-.38$, $p < .05$ and .01, respectively. Thus, girls tended not to like arousable children (regardless of sex) as much as those who were less arousable. For boys, no significant relations were found.

Sociometric Judgments and Social Behavior. Boys and girls appeared to be differentially responsive to the different social behaviors exhibited by other children. Specifically, girls' other-sex sociometric ratings were inversely related to boys' negative social attributes: $r(n = 41) = -.62$, $p < .001$. Additionally, girls' ratings of boys were positively correlated with boys' positive social attributes: $r(n = 41) = .43$, $p < .01$. In contrast, boys' sociometric ratings of girls were inversely related to the girls' positive social behaviors: $r(n = 42) = -.44$, $p < .01$.

Possible Significance. These results provide some initial support for the notion that differences in children's arousability and regulation are related to their peer-group preferences and sociometric judgments. Boys who were rated as being more highly arousable were those who played more often in same-sex versus other-sex groups. Similarly, Bukowski, Gauze, Hoza, and Newcomb (1993) found that boys who liked activities that required gross motor skills (rough-and-tumble play) were observed to show a stronger same-sex preference than boys less interested in these activities. In contrast, girls who disliked rough-and-tumble activities were especially likely to avoid boys. Such findings may be due to greater compatibility of physiological and behavioral responsiveness between some boys or to the fact that girls tended to report not liking those boys who were relatively highly arousable and, thus, may not have allowed arousable boys to play with them. Therefore, it may be important for researchers to consider that children's observed playgroup preferences represent more than whom the children like to play with; they may also indicate the degree to which children are invited or allowed to play with peers (see Chapter Three).

Our data also support the notion that boys and girls are differentially responsive to different social characteristics. Those children who tended to play more often (or were allowed to play more often) with girls were those who were rated as possessing relatively higher levels of the positive social behaviors. It may be that girls found these qualities particularly attractive or compatible whereas boys did not (although boys did not appear to find these characteristics particularly aversive either). Thus, like the data presented in Figure 2.2, our data here suggested that the girls were particularly responsive to sympathy-related conditions and characteristics, whereas the boys were not.

In our work, Eisenberg and I have found that children who are responsive to sympathetic-inducing contexts tend to be well regulated in regard to their emotional responding and their behavior in social interactions. For example, children who tend to assist others spontaneously also tend to be emotionally expressive in response to peers' behaviors and are rated by others as highly competent in their social interactions (see Eisenberg and Fabes, 1992, for a review). If, as hypothesized, girls are more optimally regulated than are boys in the context of evocative social interactions, their preferences for prosocial behaviors may be due in part to their increased regulatory competencies.

A second possible explanation of these data is that, because the qualities rated in the positive social behavior index are traditionally identified as feminine, there may have been a tendency for these children to play with girls because the girls evidenced behaviors and characteristics that were more traditionally typed as feminine. Once again, however, the question as to whether boys who were rated high in the positive social qualities chose to play with girls and/or were rejected or ignored by other boys remains unanswered.

Together, the new data presented in this chapter are highly suggestive of a relationship between children's arousability and their peer-group preferences. However, these data also have important limitations. Teacher report indexes of children's arousability and social behaviors have limited usefulness due to the relatively restricted contexts in which teachers observe their children. Because of their concerns about group cooperation and compliance, teachers may identify as arousable those children who possess qualities most likely to disrupt classroom activities (for example, high activity levels or aggressiveness). Moreover, the index of arousability is a composite index that may not assess the constructs of interest as directly as necessary, particularly in regard to arousal regulation. Clearly, there is a need for more sophisticated and direct measures of boys' and girls' arousal-related responses.

Conclusion

In the end, the question I began with remains to be definitively answered. Are there differences in emotional arousal and regulation that differentiate the sexes and cause children to find same-sex peers more attractive and compatible? According to the research reviewed and presented here, it appears that differences in the contexts that elicit arousal in boys and girls and in boys' and girls' arousal-related responses may contribute to gender segregation. If this is so, however, one must be able to explain the fact that gender segregation appears to increase with age (Maccoby and Jacklin, 1987; Whiting and Edwards, 1988). Is there also evidence that gender differences in arousability and regulation increase with age?

Block and Block (1980) report finding a trend toward increasing gender differences in ego-control and ego-resiliency (which generally map on well to the constructs of emotional arousal and regulation) from preschool to elementary school years. Moreover, Block (1976) concluded that, with increasing age, there is increasing evidence of sex differentiation. Cairns and Cairns (1984) found evidence of increasing gender differentiation in aggressive behavior as children grew older. Terman and Tyler (1954) also concluded that there is evidence for increasing sex differentiation with age in the areas of abilities, interests, preferences, and personality. Thus, there is a basis to expect that, with increasing age, there may be increasing arousal-related differences between males and females that contribute to increased gender segregation (and vice versa). However, whether these developmental changes exist and whether they contribute to gender segregation are empirical questions that have yet to be adequately addressed. Moreover, our research raises other questions to be addressed: for example, Why did the boys not like, and not play with, arousable girls? Why did the most arousable boys not choose to play with boys? Certainly, processes other than arousal-related responses—such as cognitive (Chapter Three), adult socialization (Maccoby, 1988), and peer-group processes (Chapters One, Four, and Five)—contribute to, reinforce, and strengthen (or weaken) gender segregation. However, a better understanding of the sources of gender segregation requires study of all related factors, including those involving differential physiological responsiveness and the contexts that elicit these responses.

Notes

1. At least in adults, there is some evidence that sympathy-inducing contexts are less evocative than distress-inducing contexts. Specifically, skin conductance responses occur with more frequency and with greater intensity under distress- than sympathy-inducing contexts (see Eisenberg and others, 1991b).

References

Asher, S. R., Singleton, L. C., Tinsley, B. R., and Hymel, S. "A Reliable Sociometric Measure for Preschool Children." *Developmental Psychology,* 1979, *15,* 443–444.

Bem, S. L. *The Bem Sex-Role Inventory: A Professional Manual.* Palo Alto, Calif.: Consulting Psychologists Press, 1981.

Block, J. H. "Issues, Problems, and Pitfalls in Assessing Sex Differences: A Critical Review of *The Psychology of Sex Differences.*" *Merrill-Palmer Quarterly,* 1976, *22,* 283–308.

Block, J. H., and Block, J. "The Role of Ego-control and Ego-resiliency in the Organization of Behavior." In W. A. Collins (ed.), *Development of Cognition, Affect, and Social Relations: Minnesota Symposium on Child Psychology.* Vol. 13. Hillsdale, N.J.: Erlbaum, 1980.

Blurton-Jones, N. "Categories of Child-Child Interaction." In N. Blurton-Jones (ed.), *Ethological Studies of Child Behavior.* Cambridge, England: Cambridge University Press, 1972.

Brodzinsky, D. M., Elias, M. J., Steiger, C., Simon, J., Gill, M., and Hitt, J. C. "Coping Scale for Children and Youth: Scale Development and Validation." *Journal of Applied Developmental Psychology,* 1992, *13,* 195–214.

Bukowski, W. H., Gauze, C., Hoza, B., and Newcomb, A. F. "Differences and Consistency Between Same-Sex and Other-Sex Peer Relationships During Early Adolescence." *Developmental Psychology,* 1993, *29,* 255–263.

Buss, A. H., and Plomin, R. *Temperament: Early Developing Personality Traits.* Hillsdale, N.J.: Erlbaum, 1984.

Cairns, R. B., and Cairns, B. D. "Predicting Aggressive Patterns in Girls and Boys: A Developmental Study." *Aggressive Behavior,* 1984, *10,* 227–242.

Cramer, P. "Defense Mechanisms in Adolescence." *Developmental Psychology,* 1979, *15,* 476–477.

Davis, M. "Perinatal Sex Differences in Physiological and Behavioral Stress Reactivity." Paper presented at the biennial meeting of the Society for Research in Child Development, Seattle, Mar. 1991.

DiPietro, J. A. "Rough and Tumble Play: A Function of Gender." *Developmental Psychology,* 1981, *17,* 50–58.

Eisenberg, N., and Fabes, R. A. "Emotion, Regulation, and the Development of Social Competence." In M. S. Clark (ed.), *Emotion and Social Behavior.* Vol. 14. Newbury Park, Calif.: Sage, 1992.

Eisenberg, N., Fabes, R. A., Bernzweig, J., Karbon, M., Poulin, R., and Hanish, L. "The Relations of Emotionality and Regulation to Preschoolers' Social Skills and Sociometric Status." *Child Development,* in press.

Eisenberg, N., Fabes, R. A., Nyman, M., Bernzweig, J., and Pinneulas, A. "The Relations of Emotionality and Regulation to Children's Anger-related Reactions." *Child Development,* 1994, *65,* 109–128.

Eisenberg, N., Fabes, R. A., Schaller, M., Carlo, G., and Miller, P. "The Relations of Parental Characteristics and Practices to Children's Vicarious Emotional Responding." *Child Development,* 1991a, *62,* 1393–1408.

Eisenberg, N., Fabes, R. A., Schaller, M., Miller, P., Carlo, G., Poulin, R., Shea, C., and Shell, R. "Personality and Socialization Correlates of Vicarious Emotional Responding." *Journal of Personality and Social Psychology,* 1991b, *61,* 459–470.

Erskine, M. S., Stern, J. M., and Levine, S. "Effects of Prepubertal Handling on Shock-Induced Fighting and ACTH in Male and Female Rats." *Physiology and Behavior,* 1975, *14,* 413–420.

Fabes, R. A., and Eisenberg, N. "Young Children's Coping with Interpersonal Anger." *Child Development,* 1992, *63,* 116–128.

Fabes, R. A., Eisenberg, N., and Eisenbud, L. "Physiological and Behavior Correlates of Children's Reactions to Others in Distress." *Developmental Psychology,* 1993, *29,* 655–663.

Fabes, R. A., Eisenberg, N., Karbon, M., Bernzweig, J., Speer, A. L., and Carlo, G. "Socialization of Children's Vicarious Emotional Responding and Prosocial Behavior: Relations with Mothers' Perceptions of Children's Emotional Reactivity." *Developmental Psychology,* 1994, *30,* 44–55.

Fagot, B. I. "Beyond the Reinforcement Principle: Another Step Toward Understanding Sex Roles." *Developmental Psychology,* 1985, *21,* 1097–1104.

Frankenhaeuser, M. "Challenge-Control Interaction as Reflected in Sympathetic-Adrenal and Pituitary-Adrenal Activity: Comparison Between the Sexes." *Scandinavian Journal of Psychology,* 1982, *71,* 158–164.

Frankenhaeuser, M., Rauste-von Wright, M., Collins, A., von Wright, J., Sedvall, G., and Swahn, C. G. "Sex Differences in Psychoneuroendocrine Reactions to Examination Stress." *Psychosomatic Medicine,* 1978, *40,* 334–343.

Gottman, J. M., and Levenson, R. W. "The Social Psychophysiology of Marriage." In P. Noller and M. A. Fitzpatrick (eds.), *Perspectives on Marital Interaction.* Philadelphia: Multilingual Matters, 1988.

Gray, J. *The Psychology of Fear and Stress.* New York: McGraw-Hill, 1971.

Gunnar-Gnechten, M. R. "Changing a Frightening Toy into a Pleasant One by Allowing the Infant to Control It." *Developmental Psychology,* 1978, *14,* 157–162.

Haviland, J. J., and Malatesta, C. Z. "The Development of Sex Differences in Nonverbal Signals: Fallacies, Facts, and Fantasies." In C. Mayo and N. M. Henley (eds.), *Gender and Nonverbal Behavior.* New York: Springer-Verlag, 1981.

Hoyenga, K. B., and Hoyenga, K. T. *The Question of Sex Differences.* Boston: Little, Brown, 1979.

Larsen, R. J., Diener, E., and Emmons, R. A. "Affect Intensity and Reactions to Daily Life Events." *Journal of Personality and Social Psychology,* 1986, *51,* 803–804.

Lazarus, R. S., and Folkman, S. *Stress, Appraisal, and Coping.* New York: Springer, 1984.

Leaper, C. "Influence and Involvement in Children's Discourse: Age, Gender, and Partner Effects." *Child Development,* 1991, *62,* 797–811.

Maccoby, E. E. "Gender as a Social Category." *Developmental Psychology,* 1988, *24,* 755–765.

Maccoby, E. E. "Gender and Relationships: A Developmental Account." *American Psychologist,* 1990, *45* (4), 513–520.

Maccoby, E. E., and Jacklin, C. N. "Gender Segregation in Childhood." In H. W. Reese (ed.), *Advances in Child Development and Behavior.* Vol. 20. New York: Academic Press, 1987.

Maltz, D. N., and Borker, R. A. "A Cultural Approach to Male-Female Miscommunication." In J. J. Gumperz (ed.), *Language and Social Identity.* New York: Cambridge University Press, 1982.

Marcus, J., Maccoby, E. E., Jacklin, C. N., and Doering, C. H. "Individual Differences in Mood: Their Relation to Gender and Neonatal Sex Steroids." *Developmental Psychobiology,* 1985, *18,* 327–340.

Meany, M. J., Stewart, J., and Beatty, W. W. "Sex Differences in Social Play: The Socialization of Sex Roles." In J. S. Rosenblatt, C. Bear, C. M. Busnell, and P. Slater (eds.), *Advances in the Study of Behavior.* Vol. 15. San Diego: Academic Press, 1985.

Miller, P. M., Danaher, D. L., and Forbes, D. "Sex-Related Strategies for Coping with Interpersonal Conflict in Children Aged Five and Seven." *Developmental Psychology,* 1986, *22,* 543–548.

Moss, H. A. "Early Sex Differences and Mother-Infant Interaction." In R. C. Feldman, R. M. Richart, and R. L. Wiele (eds.), *Sex Differences in Behavior.* New York: Wiley, 1974.

Nolen-Hoeksema, S. "Sex Differences in Responses to Depression." Paper presented at the annual meeting of the American Psychological Association, San Francisco, Aug. 1991.

Pulkkinen, L. "Self-control and Continuity from Childhood to Adolescence." In P. B. Baltes and O. G. Brim (eds.), *Life-span Development and Behavior.* Vol. 4. San Diego: Academic Press, 1982.

Rauste-von Wright, M., von Wright, J., and Frankenhaeuser, M. "Relationships Between Sex-related Psychological Characteristics During Adolescence and Catecholamine Excretion During Achievement Stress." *Psychophysiology,* 1981, *18,* 362–370.

Rothbart, M. K., and Derryberry, D. "Development of Individual Differences in Temperament." In M. E. Lamb and A. L. Brown (eds.), *Advances in Developmental Psychology.* Vol. 1. Hillsdale, N.J.: Erlbaum, 1981.

Rothbart, M. K., Ziaie, H., and O'Boyle, C. G. "Self-Regulation and Emotion in Infancy." In N. Eisenberg and R. A. Fabes (eds.), *Emotion and Its Regulation in Early Development.* New Directions for Child Development, no. 55. San Francisco: Jossey-Bass, 1992.

Savin-Williams, R. C. "Dominance Hierarchies in Groups of Early Adolescents." *Child Development,* 1979, *50,* 923–935.

Serbin, L. A., Sprafkin, C., Elman, M., and Doyle, A. B. "The Early Development of Sex Differentiated Patterns of Social Influence." *Canadian Journal of Social Science,* 1982, *14* (4) 350–363.

Suomi, S. J. "Development of Attachment and Other Social Behaviors in Rhesus Monkeys." In T. Alloway, P. Piner, and L. Kranes (eds.), *Attachment Behavior.* Vol. 3. New York: Plenum, 1977.

Terman, L. M., and Tyler, L. E. "Psychological Sex Differences." In L. Carmichael (ed.), *Manual of Child Psychology.* New York: Wiley, 1954.

Thorne, B. "Girls and Boys Together, but Mostly Apart." In W. W. Hartup and Z. Rubin (eds.), *Relationship and Development.* Hillsdale, N.J.: Erlbaum, 1986.

Whiting, B. B., and Edwards, C. P. *Children of Different Worlds.* Cambridge, Mass.: Harvard University Press, 1988.

Zaslow, M. J., and Hayes, C. D. "Sex Differences in Children's Response to Psychosocial Stress: Toward a Cross-Context Analysis." In M. E. Lamb, A. L. Brown, and B. Rogoff (eds.), *Advances in Developmental Psychology.* Vol. 4. Hillsdale, N.J.: Erlbaum, 1986.

RICHARD A. FABES is associate professor of child development in the Department of Family Resources and Human Development at Arizona State University, Tempe.

Both children's explicit gender knowledge and implicit theories of gender can be profitably examined as part of a cognitive approach to the development and maintenance of gender segregation.

Cognitive Influences on the Development and Maintenance of Gender Segregation

Carol Lynn Martin

A visit to any school playground is sufficient to illustrate one of the most consistent patterns found in the developmental literature, namely, that girls prefer to play with girls and boys prefer to play with boys. Such gender segregation has been described as one of the most powerful developmental phenomena because it occurs so frequently and increases as children grow older. Because girls and boys play differently, to the extent that children maintain gender-segregated playgroups, girls and boys are exposed to different social environments. A better understanding of why gender segregation occurs is important because these environments are training grounds for learning how to interact with others and perform various skills.

Much of the research on gender segregation has focused on how the actual qualities of, and differences in, girls' and boys' play patterns may contribute to gender segregation. The goal of this chapter is different. I ask whether children are aware of these qualities and whether their knowledge about other children and what other children do influences gender segregation. Thus, my approach is cognitive. Specifically, I consider the role of cognitive factors in three very broad areas: how gender segregation begins, how it is maintained, and what its variations are. (Because of space limitations, only brief reviews of the relevant research on gender segregation are presented.)

Characteristics of Cognitive Approaches

The assumption underlying cognitive approaches is that individuals play an active role in interpreting information from their environments. They are not

NEW DIRECTIONS FOR CHILD DEVELOPMENT, no. 65, Fall 1994 © Jossey-Bass Publishers passive recipients of information; instead, they use "theories" to interpret information, and in doing so, they create environments supportive of their theories (Martin and Halverson, 1987). Research based on cognitive approaches has focused on nature of the theories that individuals hold and on the influence these theories have on the kinds of information individuals perceive, attend to, and remember.

Among the offshoots of the cognitive approach have been gender schema theories. Three of these theories have been proposed in recent years (Bem, 1981; Markus, Crane, Bernstein, and Siladi, 1982; Martin and Halverson, 1981), and although similar in many ways, they vary by emphasizing either the ways individuals, especially adults, differ in their use of gender schemas (Bem, 1981; Markus, Crane, Bernstein, and Siladi, 1982) or the developmental changes in these schemas and their resulting functions and biases (Martin and Halverson, 1981, 1987). Although the exact nature of gender schemas has not yet been determined, the working assumption is that children and adults do have clearly defined and well-organized knowledge structures about what the sexes are like. (However, the label "knowledge structures" does not imply that the information in these structures is accurate. In fact, most cognitive theorists believe that these structures contain information that goes beyond how the sexes differ.) Thus, these schemas provide the knowledge bases that motivate, guide, and structure the way individuals view and interpret events in their worlds. Essentially, the schemas act as filters for perception, such that individuals often see what they expect to see rather than what is really there. They also act as organizers for memory by providing a structure to help encode and retain information. Not all researchers agree with these ideas about the roles of schemas. In particular, the extent to which cognitive knowledge underlies behavior has been questioned (see Huston, 1985; Martin, 1993). Nevertheless, although many of these issues are still being sorted out, it is still useful to consider when and how cognitions may influence gender segregation.

Types of Gender Knowledge

An individual's gender knowledge may exist in more than one type of schema and may also be explicit or abstract.

Explicit Gender Knowledge. One kind of explicit gender knowledge is the *superordinate schema,* which consists of all the general information children need to enable them to categorize objects, behaviors, traits, and roles as related to either females or males. The superordinate schema could be called a gender stereotype, because it consists of list-like information about characteristics associated with each sex (for example, that boys like to play with trucks). This schema is assumed to be hierarchically organized. The top level includes category labels, such as female and male, and the lower levels include gender-related attributes: for example, has long hair, likes to play football (see Martin, 1993; Martin, Wood, and Little, 1990). Category labels are presumed to organize the information within the structure (Fagot, 1985). The attributes associated with the labels may also be organized into components, such as role behaviors, occupations, traits, and physical appearance (Deaux and Lewis, 1984; Martin, Wood, and Little, 1990). The concepts of masculinity and femininity link together information within and between various components and between the labels and attributes.

A second kind of explicit gender knowledge is contained in the *own-sex schema,* a subordinate schema that is a narrower and more detailed version of the first, containing detailed plans of action for carrying out traditionally sex-typed behavior. For instance, because sewing is typically considered sex-typed for girls, girls may then learn the action patterns involved in sewing better than boys (Martin and Halverson, 1981, 1987). Recent research has supported this idea: children learn more quickly the ordering of events sex-typed for their sex than those sex-typed for the other sex (Boston and Levy, 1991; Levy and Fivush, 1993).

Children may also develop the flip-side of the own-sex schema, that is, the *other-sex schema,* which contains plans of action for activities sex-typed for the other sex (Martin, 1991). The amount of detail in the own-sex versus the other-sex schema likely depends on the degree to which children identify with their own gender group. For many children raised to identify with their own sex, one would expect highly elaborated own-sex schemas and much less elaborated other-sex schemas. Other children, "tomboys" for example, may have equally elaborated own- and other-sex schemas. Children with gender identity disorders may identify with the other sex and thus form extensive other-sex schemas while not elaborating their own-sex schemas.

Abstract Gender Knowledge. Most of the work on cognitive approaches has emphasized the role of the explicit knowledge individuals have about gender. Less emphasis has been given to the more abstract, or implicit, theories of gender that individuals also seem to form. For instance, children may assume similarity between themselves and others of their own sex based not particularly on specific information about similarity but rather on a more abstract notion that "others of my sex are like me." One goal of this chapter is to consider the contributions of both explicit and abstract gender knowledge to the development and maintenance of gender segregation.

Development of Gender Segregation

The extremity of gender segregation in preschoolers and in older children (see Hartup, 1983; Carter, 1987; Maccoby, 1988, for reviews) has been well documented, but much less is known about when gender segregation first begins. In one large-scale study of 142 Quebecois children ranging in age from one to six years old, LaFreniere, Strayer, and Gauthier (1984) found that the youngest children (mean age = seventeen months) showed no tendency to focus their affiliative acts (for example, approaches and contact) to same-sex over other-sex peers. By twenty-seven months, however, children did begin to show a same-sex pattern of responses. A sex difference was also found: girls showed the same-sex bias in affiliative responses before boys, but by thirty-six months, both sexes showed similar same-sex biases. The tendency for same-sex biases to emerge slowly from about seventeen months to three years has been confirmed in several other studies by contributors to this volume (see Chapters One and Four). Others have shown that gender segregation is commonly found in three-year-old children (Charlesworth and Hartup, 1967; Serbin, Tonick, and Sternglanz, 1977). Fabes (Chapter Two) found gender-segregated play over 60 percent of the time in preschool children.

Behavioral Compatibility. What factors account for this change in toddlers' behavior? (Because the factors that influence the emergence of gender segregation may not be the same as those that influence the strengthening of gender segregation with age, it is important to consider research that has dealt specifically with toddlers.) One factor that contributes to the emergence of gender segregation is behavioral compatibility, that is, the notion that the sexes may have different interests or may behave differently, and these interests or behaviors may attract others of the same sex (Chapters One and Five; Goodenough, 1934). For example, among toddlers, boys spend more time in negative interactions than girls (Chapter Four). Boys also engage in more rough-and-tumble play, and girls, when in mixed pairs, seem to withdraw from this sort of play (Jacklin and Maccoby, 1978).

One striking finding is that when segregating and nonsegregating children are compared, segregating girls engage in more socially skilled play than other girls, while segregating boys engage in less socially skilled play than other boys. Thus, gender segregation in toddlers may relate to sex-differentiated styles of interaction (see Chapter One). In addition, also among toddlers, same-sex groups have a higher quality of play than mixed-sex groups (Chapter One) and more social behavior overall (Jacklin and Maccoby, 1978). These studies were carried out with white, middle-class samples; in a study with slightly older black children, more social behavior was found among boys in mixed-sex groups (Langlois, Gottfried, and Seay, 1973). Also, children are more likely to engage in cooperative play than parallel play in same-sex groups, indicating that play in same-sex groups may be more developmentally advanced than in mixed-sex groups (Chapter One).

Influence of Gender Stereotypes. How may gender-related cognitions influence the initial development of gender segregation? Very young children have rudimentary forms of stereotypical knowledge; for instance, three-year-olds report that girls cry a lot and boys hit people (Kuhn, Nash, and Brucken, 1978). One might expect that when children begin acquiring this kind of information that it would influence whom they chose to play with. In a study with a large age range of children (from thirty-nine to eighty-two months), Levy and Barth (1990) found that stereotyped knowledge of activities, occupations, and objects correlated with interaction with same-sex peers. When only toddlers have been studied, however, their knowledge of sex-typed activities does not seem to relate to gender segregation (Chapter One).

There are a number of possible explanations why superordinate schema information such as knowledge about sex-typed activities may not relate to behavior for very young children. First, young children seem to pay attention, in general, more to the categories of gender than they do to specific attributes associated with those categories (Berndt and Heller, 1986; Biernat, 1991; Martin, 1989b). That is, they seem to base their judgments of others on sex rather than on other more specific information, even when they know it. In one of my previous studies, four- to ten-year olds were asked how much they would like unfamiliar children, predicting how much these children would like various masculine and feminine toys (Martin, 1989b). For instance, they made judgments about a boy who was said to like playing with airplanes (a stereotypical interest) and a boy who was said to like playing with kitchen sets (a counter-stereotypical interest). The youngest children showed an interesting pattern: they virtually ignored information about interests and decided how much they would like the unfamiliar child (and rated toys the child would like) based only on the child's sex. Older children's judgments were somewhat modified by the additional information they were given about the child's interests (Martin, 1989b). The explanation for these findings is unclear, but they do suggest that gender is extremely salient for young children and may overwhelm other information. Although no research has specifically tested this notion with toddlers, one might expect this tendency to use sex rather than other information to be even stronger for younger children.

Before the idea that gender stereotype knowledge relates to gender segregation is abandoned, it is necessary also to consider how specific items of knowledge rather than the level of general knowledge may relate to actual behavior. A girl who believes that girls help people more than boys do may prefer girls more than a girl does who has not formed this particular belief. Therefore, it may be necessary to assess children's beliefs about specific play qualities exhibited by girls and boys to find the kinds of knowledge that best predict actual play behavior. Such an assessment is described later in this chapter.

Influence of Gender Labeling. In terms of cognitions that may influence the initiation of gender segregation, a more likely candidate than stereotypes is children's knowledge of their own gender group. As Maccoby and Jacklin (1987) state, "the mere fact of knowing that one is a boy or girl might lead a child to prefer other children known to be similar to the self" (p. 252). These cognitions may be virtually universal, and as such, their role in gender segregation may be quite powerful (Maccoby, 1988, 1990; Maccoby and Jacklin, 1987); they may be the "primary cognitive underpinnings" of gender segregation (Maccoby, 1988, p. 755).

Presumably, once children can label their own gender group and the other gender group, this knowledge helps them organize other information they have about the sexes and, thus, is more likely to relate to their behavior. Several studies confirm this notion. Fagot and her colleagues have found in two studies, one with twenty- to thirty-month-olds (Fagot, 1985) and one with twenty-one- to forty-month-olds (Fagot, Leinbach, and Hagan, 1986), that toddlers who show the ability to label the sexes spend more time with same-sex peers than those who have not yet attained this ability. These results are in contrast to the findings discussed in Chapter One, but the discrepancy may be due to the high levels of accuracy in gender labeling among the toddlers in that study.

Early gender cognitions, even those represented only by the ability to label the sexes, are likely to work their influence through broad-based and abstract theories about the sexes. Once children can reliably label the sexes, a wide variety of group-related behaviors are assumed to be initiated, such as preferences for one's own group over other groups, preferences for things one's own group does over things other groups do, and general tendencies to be biased in favor of one's own group (Fagot, 1985; Maccoby, 1988; Maccoby and Jacklin, 1987; Martin and Halverson, 1981). These group-based processes have been described for a wide variety of groups, even arbitrarily defined groups (Duveen and Lloyd, 1986; Tajfel, 1981; Wilder and Allen, 1974). It is known, for instance, that merely labeling groups can lead to the exaggeration of group differences (Tajfel, 1981).

What sets these group processes in motion? One way to address this question is to assess the nature of the beliefs that underlie groups and that must trigger these group processes. At the most basic level, these beliefs might be simply two theories, one concerning group differences and one concerning within-group similarity. For instance, imagine a young boy given an attractive novel toy, one he does not know to be sex-linked. If he likes the toy, and if he holds these abstract theories, he may predict that other boys would like the toy and other girls would not. The basis of the prediction for other boys is the belief that there is some underlying essence or basic similarity (see Medin, 1989) that links all boys together. The basis of the prediction for girls is the belief that girls do not share this essence of "boyness" and so their preferences must be different than those of boys.

A Study of Children's Abstract Gender Theories. Lisa Eisenbud, Hilary Rose, and I (Martin, Eisenbud, and Rose, under review) have done research to determine whether or not the two abstract theories just described are used by children. In two studies, preschoolers (n = 22 and 71, respectively), were asked to help us decide how much other children would like a variety of highly and moderately attractive unfamiliar toys. Children rated how much they like each toy, how much they thought other girls would like each toy, and how much they thought other boys would like each toy. Children's abstract theories influenced their predictions. They did not believe that boys and girls would like the same toys. More importantly, when asked about unfamiliar toys, the children who liked an unfamiliar toy predicted that peers of the same sex would also like the toy while peers of the other sex would not.

Abstract gender theories could easily bias children's peer preferences. Children who hold these abstract beliefs might reason that others of the same sex are "like me" and thus more fun to play with (no matter what they are doing), while peers of the other sex are "not like me" and, thus, less fun to play with (no matter what they are doing). In this way, sex can be used as a marker of expected similarities. Furthermore, to the extent that children hold these abstract theories of within-group similarity and between-group differences, they need not experience actual compatibility in interests or play styles to be motivated to engage in gender segregation. Instead, they merely need to presume similarity to push them into own-sex groups. Moreover, they merely need to presume dissimilarity to push them away from other-sex groups. Actual compatibility in interests or in play styles may provide additional evidence of the adequacy of their theories but would not be a necessary prerequisite for gender segregation.

Additional research is needed to more clearly elaborate the full range of factors that contribute to early gender segregation in toddlers. At this point, it is unclear whether gender cognitions set gender segregation in motion or whether the cognitions develop concurrently but independently from gender segregation (see Chapter One). Furthermore, to better understand the role of cognition, we need to focus more attention on younger children and infants. It may be the case that we have not yet found methods sensitive enough to detect very young children's gender knowledge. For instance, when new methods of assessing gender knowledge have been used, a set of intriguing findings emerge: even nine-month-olds seem to have formed categories about males and females (Leinbach and Fagot, 1993; Poulin-Dubois, Serbin, Kenyon, and Derbyshire, 1992). These categories may lay the groundwork for the development of gender knowledge, and although it is highly speculative at this early stage of research, it is possible that this rudimentary gender knowledge may play a role in the formation of gender-segregated groups among toddlers.

Maintenance and Development of Gender Segregation

As children grow older, gender segregation increases. Among children from four and one-half to six and one-half years of age, it has been found that the younger children interacted with same-sex peers three times more often than with other-sex peers while the older group interacted with same-sex peers eleven times more often than with other-sex peers (Maccoby and Jacklin, 1987; Maccoby, 1988). For these children, however, tendencies to play with same-sex peers were not found to be consistent over the span of a week. When asked about playmates, children express preferences for affiliating with unfamiliar same-sex peers more than with other-sex peers, and these preferences increase from preschool through elementary school (Carter and McCloskey, 1984; Martin, 1989b; Serbin, Powlishta, and Gulko, 1993; Serbin and Sprafkin, 1986). Older children continue to show gender-related preferences and their preferences remain consistent over time (Bukowski, Gauze, Hoza, and Newcomb, 1993). Similarly, in children's reports concerning their close relationships, they also show preferences for the same sex (Rubin, 1980).

Behavioral Compatibility and Dominance Relations. Behavioral compatibility may account for the maintenance and strengthening of gender segregation. Play patterns and behavior continue to be different for boys and girls (see Chapter Five). Boys are more likely to play competitively outdoors, and girls are more likely to play cooperatively indoors (Stoneman, Brody, and MacKinnon, 1984).

Girls and boys also maintain and strengthen their different styles of influence. As girls grow older, they increase their use of polite suggestions whereas boys use more direct demands and become less responsive to polite suggestion (Leaper, 1991; Serbin, Sprafkin, Elman, and Doyle, 1982). In mixed groups, boys are more likely to "get their way" in terms of obtaining access to scarce resources (Charlesworth and LaFreniere, 1983; LaFreniere and Charlesworth, 1987), although the sex difference in access to scarce resources disappears when an adult is present (Powlishta and Maccoby, 1990). It is likely that one factor leading to the increase in gender segregation in older children is the changing nature of the dominance relations between the sexes (Maccoby and Jacklin, 1987). Another influential factor is the way in which other children interpret behavior occurring across gender groups. Among older children, play with other-sex peers is often a basis for teasing about romantic involvement (Chapter Five; Thorne, 1986).

In adopting a cognitive approach, it is important to reexamine ideas about behavioral compatibility from the perspective of children's beliefs about their social environments. Specifically, in addition to assessing the actual qualities of children's playgroups, cognitive theorists are interested in whether children know about these differences in play quality. For instance, do girls know that boys are more likely to engage in rough-and-tumble play than girls? And, if they know this, does it decrease girls' desire to join boys' groups? Are girls aware of their lack of influence over boys and do they avoid boys because of being unable to exert control during play? As children grow older, they might be expected to learn more and more about the play qualities of girl and boy groups, and such explicit gender knowledge about playgroups may increase children's tendencies to gender segregate as they grow older. The study described later in this chapter also addresses these questions.

Changes in Gender Knowledge. Gender knowledge changes as children grow older, and these changes may influence children's gender segregation. One change is simply that children have more information in their stereotypes about the sexes. For instance, at a young age, children learn about the activities associated with the sexes but only around the age of ten or eleven do they begin to associate subtle personality stereotypes with the sexes (for example, that females are sympathetic) (see Huston, 1983, for review). Another change is that children begin to develop the more complex associations between and within the various content domains linked with gender labels. Moreover, there is also evidence suggesting that children's ideas about the sexes become more extreme as children grow older. Specifically, older children predict that girls and boys will differ more drastically in their interests than younger children will predict, especially when there is no firm evidence provided about actual interests (Martin, 1989b).

With their increased knowledge about the sexes, older children also develop understanding about gender-role flexibility (Stoddard and Turiel, 1985). For instance, older children are more likely than younger children to acknowledge that some children engage in cross-sex activities (Leahy and Shirk, 1984). However, surprisingly, just as they seem to acquire this flexibility they also become less tolerant in some ways. Very young children, who seem to associate cross-sex dress with threats to gender identity, react negatively to such behavior, as do adolescents who view it as deviant behavior (Stoddard and Turiel, 1985). Also, as children grow older, their reactions to cross-sex activities and friendships become more negative (Carter and McCloskey, 1984). Thus, older children may hold a complex set of beliefs: they may understand more about the actual behavior of both girls and boys, but they may also understand more about the social consequences, especially rejection, associated with some cross-sex behaviors (see Serbin, Powlishta, and Gulko, 1993; Signorella, Bigler, and Liben, 1993; Stoddard and Turiel, 1985). Thus, they may steer away from cross-sex behaviors and from interactions with the other sex.

A Study of Children's Knowledge of Play Qualities and Consequences. In a large-scale study of gender segregation and social behavior in preschoolers, Richard Fabes, Nancy Eisenberg, and I have been investigating some of the cognitive contributors to gender segregation. For one aspect of the study, we interviewed children (n = 52, forty-one to seventy-seven months old, mean age = sixty-two months) to determine their stated and actual playmate preferences, their sociometric status, what they know about the qualities of play with girls versus boys, and whether they have ideas about others' approval or disapproval for play partner selection. We were also interested in assessing their abstract theories about gender groups. Specifically, we assessed their ideas about who other girls and boys most like to play with.

Playmate Preferences. In our study, we collected multiple measures on play, including observation data and sociometric information about peers. We also collected self-report data: children rated how much they would like to play with girls and with boys and how much they actually play with girls and with boys (on a scale from 1 to 3).

Thus far, we have concentrated our analyses on the children's self-reports of peer preferences and liking of girls and boys. Not surprisingly, both boys and girls showed a strong same-sex bias in reporting whom they would prefer to play with and whom they actually play with, saying they preferred to play with both same-sex individuals and groups more than other-sex individuals and groups (see Table 3.1). They also reported that they actually play with same-sex more than other-sex peers ($p < .001$). About 65 percent of the sample said they play with same-sex peers and avoid other-sex peers, 24 percent said they play with both boys and girls, and 10 percent said they play with other-sex more than with same-sex peers.

These self-report measures led us to reconsider how gender segregation is conceptualized. For gender segregation to occur, two things must typically

Table 3.1. Girls' and Boys' Playmate Preferences

	Girls	Boys
Like to play with:		
Individual girl	2.71	1.84
Group of girls	2.82	1.83
Individual boy	2.19	2.88
Group of boys	2.19	2.80
Observed to play with:		
Boys	1.94	2.68
Girls	2.80	1.92

Note: Ratings are on a scale from 1 to 3.

happen. First, a child must show interest in playing with a same-sex group. Second, the child must be accepted by the group. By focusing on children's play, researchers have assumed that children's actual play partners match their desired play partners. But this may not be true. For instance, some girls may desire to play with boys but not be accepted into any boy groups.

We examined children's self-report data to explore this issue, and found that, for same-sex playgroups, most children in the sample (80 percent) reported that they both liked same-sex peers and that they played in same-sex groups. Out of those who said they liked same-sex peers a lot, 20 percent were rejected by same-sex groups (that is, they said they did not play with same-sex peers a lot). For other-sex playgroups, the pattern was different. Many children (46 percent) said that they did not like other-sex children and that they did not play with them often. However, rejection occurred much more often with other-sex groups: 47 percent of children who liked other-sex peers said they did not play with them much. These findings suggest that it is useful to consider that some children may desire to play with other-sex groups but are not allowed to (rejected children), whereas others may both desire to play with other-sex groups and be allowed to (accepted children). Thus, gender segregation is not entirely up to the target child—it is not simply a preference being expressed. Often information about gender segregation is reported as "choice of play partners" when this is only part of what determines play patterns (see, also, Bukowski, Gauze, Hoza, and Newcomb, 1993). More research is needed to investigate the possibility of distinguishing between desired and actual play with others. One possible advantage to this distinction is that it may increase researchers' ability to predict individual differences in gender segregation.

Beliefs About Play with Boys and Girls. To assess children's beliefs about play with girls and boys, we showed children pictures of unfamiliar children in four different types of playgroups: one girl, one boy, three girls, and three boys (picture order was varied). The purpose of varying the number of children was to assess whether children's beliefs about the sexes might relate more to groups than to individuals. For example, would children be more likely to attribute chasing to boy groups rather than to individual boys? Our major goal

**Table 3.2. Percentages of Girls and Boys Who Sex-Type
Specific Characteristics**

	Boys	Girls
Masculine characteristics:		
Fights	17%	14%
Chases	50	7
Plays tricks on others	33	19
Feminine characteristics:		
Plays inside	13%	52%
Plays games with rules	8	30
Helps others	17	30

in this procedure, however, was to assess what children know about six particular play quality differences: girls' being more likely to play inside, play games with rules, and help others, and boys' being more likely to chase one another, play tricks, and fight. Presumably, gender segregation may become even stronger when children begin to attribute specific differences in play styles to each sex. Children rated each of the four playgroups on the likelihood of their having each of the six characteristics.

We were also interested in whether children would predict same-sex play partners for others, and so children made predictions about how much other girls and boys would like to play with the child or children in each picture. To assess children's sensitivity to social approval, children were also asked how much others would like it if they played with the children in the various picture.

One surprising finding was that children's beliefs about play were similar for the individual children and the groups of children. Apparently their ideas about the sexes do not change depending on whether they are considering individuals or groups.

Also, we expected to find that children would already know about the characteristics of play with girls versus play with boys. Therefore, it was another surprise to find that children's knowledge of these specific characteristics was only moderate. Generally, children knew more about the qualities of play in the same-sex groups than in other-sex groups ($p < .01$). Table 3.2 illustrates this pattern for individual items. Girls more than boys sex-typed feminine play qualities, attributing these characteristics more to girl than to boys. Boys showed the reverse pattern: masculine play qualities were attributed to boys more than to girls. Fighting was the exception. Children generally attributed very little fighting to any group.

These results concerning children's knowledge of play qualities need to be supplemented with more extensive investigations. The area most crucial to gender segregation may be the study of beliefs about highly active interactions such as rough-and-tumble play and fighting, which may be attractive for boys but not for girls (see Chapter Two). Among older children, girls who dislike rough-and-tumble play avoid friendships with boys (Bukowski, Gauze, Hoza, and Newcomb, 1993). Furthermore, girls and boys may interpret active play differently. The active interactions that boys may find interesting may be interpreted by girls as fighting rather than play, and girls may try to avoid this "fighting" by avoiding boys.

Cognitive Correlates of Children's Play Preferences. To assess the cognitive correlates of gender segregation, we examined how gender knowledge correlated with children's expressed preferences for same-sex others and with their reports of actual play partners. Children's overall knowledge of the qualities of play among boys and girls showed a weak relation to their reports of play preferences: $r(n = 43) = .19, p < .09$. The correlations with specific kinds of knowledge were somewhat higher (with age controlled). For boys, knowledge that boys fight more than girls correlated with liking of boys: $r(n = 19) = .44$, $p < .05$; and knowledge that boys chase more than girls correlated with liking of boys and playing with boys: r .40 and .41, $p < .05$. Also, knowledge that girls play inside more than boys correlated with boys not playing with girls: $r = -.40, p < .05$. For girls, there was a trend for knowledge of several of the feminine play qualities to correlate with liking and playing with same-sex others: $r(n = 24) = .32, p < .06$.

Children's expectations for approval from others correlated with play preferences, especially for boys. The more boys reported a stereotypical approval pattern (that is, that others would approve of same-sex over other-sex play), the more they said they liked boys: $r(n = 19) = .57, p < .01$; and the more they said they played with them: $r = .40, p < .05$. Similarly, the more girls reported a stereotypical approval pattern, they more they said they liked girls: $r(n = 24) = .35, p < .05$. These findings are congruent with other recent evidence suggesting that children's understanding of the approval or disapproval of others is important for guiding their behavior (see Bussey and Bandura, 1992).

Overall, the strongest correlates involved children's abstract knowledge of others' peer preferences. Children who reported the stereotypical pattern that other girls like girls more than boys (and that other boys like boys more than girls) also reported that they liked same-sex peers more than other-sex peers—girls: $r(n = 24) = .54, p < .01$; boys: $r(n = 19) = .70, p < .001$—and that they play with same-sex peers more than other-sex peer—girls: $r = .25, p < .11$; boys: $r = .37, p < .05$.

Future Research

My colleagues and I are presently collecting another round of data from children in our lab school to enlarge our data set, and we have also collected data on actual play behavior of these children, so that we will be able to assess whether the factors just described correlate with actual gender segregation. At this point, however, our results suggest at least three areas needing further exploration. The first is how gender segregation is defined. The second is children's knowledge of play qualities of girls' versus boys' groups. (Given that our sample had less than perfect knowledge, testing older children may further researchers' understanding of why gender segregation becomes stronger with age.) And the third is children's abstract ideas about gender and how they relate to play preferences.

Gender Segregation Variations

Most explanations of gender segregation have focused on the separateness of girls and boys in school situations. It is also clear, however, that gender segregation does not always occur (see Chapter Five). In some situations, neighborhoods for instance, less gender segregation occurs (Ellis, Rogoff, and Cromer, 1981). Furthermore, gender segregation occurs less often when children have fewer playmate choices (Maccoby and Jacklin, 1987) and when situations are structured around cooperative tasks (Thorne, 1986).

Some recent advances in thinking about cognitive factors seem to be particularly useful for understanding variability in gender segregation. Most importantly, cognitive theorists are now emphasizing the way knowledge structures are sensitive to the social context (Levy, 1989). They are considering when and how gender knowledge becomes salient, how situations constrain and change cognitive processing, the role of values, and the resulting influence of all these factors on behavior and thinking (see Deaux and Major, 1987; Devine, 1989; Martin, 1989a). Although these notions are still being developed, some speculation on how these factors influence gender segregation may be useful for guiding future research (Martin, 1989a).

How can variations in levels of gender segregation be cognitively explained? It is difficult to believe that children's gender labeling abilities change in different situations. Rather, it is more likely that certain aspects of situations moderate the influence of cognitive factors. Some situations are likely to increase the salience of gender, thereby increasing the likelihood of gender segregation, while other situations may decrease the salience of gender, thereby decreasing gender segregation. When teachers instruct youngsters to line up by sex, they are making gender salient. When children tease each other about romantic interests, gender is made salient. In contrast, Thorne (1986) has argued that in situations where children are highly engaged in a task or are actively cooperating, gender salience is low and gender segregation is less likely.

Children's values also likely influence gender segregation. As mentioned earlier, simply knowing whether one is a girl or boy allows the possibility of making many group-related value judgments. Because they recognize their membership in a group, children often form in-groups and out-groups, an activity that may then lead to evaluations about these groups.

Beyond change in their general evaluations, children may experience change in their specific values as they grow older or find themselves in different situations. Less gender segregation in neighborhoods may result simply from the value children place on play. It may be better to play with the other sex than with no one. Thus, children's values are fluid and situational. A young child who fears teasing about romantic encounters if caught playing with the other sex clearly does not value romance. A few years later, the same child may welcome contact with the other sex because the child then values romance and, thus, no longer fears ridicule.

Values may also help explain individual differences in gender segregation. Some children show little gender segregation; however, some of them may try to cross gender lines and be excluded, others may be included only for specific activities (playing soccer for example), and only a few may be allowed full access to cross-gender activities and playmates (Thorne, 1986). Children who show only limited interest in the other sex may be driven more by valuing specific activities than by worrying about such results as teasing. Children who show more consistent cross-gender play may have reversed the typical in-group–out-group evaluations: they may value the other group and what it does more than their own group. In these cases, the underlying cognitive processes may be the same as for other children but the context differs.

Finally, researchers need to consider how all these factors work together to influence behavior. One way to think about this is that children may engage in a cost-benefit analysis of situations to help them decide whether or not they will attempt to enter same- or other-sex playgroups. Most of the time, and for most children, little weighing of costs and benefits would occur because, when given the options of many playgroups, joining a same-sex group may be virtually automatic behavior for most children (Martin, 1989a, 1991). It is likely that only when a child wants to perturb the typical pattern will cost-benefit thinking occur. For instance, a girl who wants to join a boys' soccer game may consider the outcome of her choice in order to decide if it is worth the costs. Children who highly value a cross–sex-typed activity may be inclined to endure more teasing because the benefits they perceive to accrue from the play outweigh the perceived costs.

Conclusions

Cognitive explanations for gender segregation have been discussed as a way of supplementing, not replacing, other kinds of explanations based on children's actual play styles. My goal was to illustrate the ways in which cognitive factors may contribute to the strong and consistent patterns of gender segregation as well as to the variations in gender segregation by situation and by individuals. The strong and consistent patterns of gender segregation are probably best accounted for by a certain set of shared cognitions about children's gender groups. Both boys and girls may believe that playing with others like themselves is more fun than playing with the other sex, regardless of what activity is occurring. Both girls and boys may recognize that certain consequences are likely to occur in same-sex versus other-sex groups concerning the possibility of obtaining resources and in getting one's way. Both girls and boys tease each other when gender lines are crossed because they share beliefs about contact with the other sex. In contrast, variations in gender segregation may be accounted for by a set of individual cognitions and by situational factors. Some children may want to play a sport or a game so badly that teasing is seen as relatively unimportant. To fully understand the powerful phenomenon of gender segregation, we need to explore both the universal qualities that may underlie children's play preferences and drive them toward segregation, and the more situational and individual qualities that may dampen or reverse segregation.

References

Bem, S. L. "Gender Schema Theory: A Cognitive Account of Sex Typing." *Psychological Review,* 1981, *88,* 354–364.

Berndt, T., and Heller, K. A. "Gender Stereotypes and Social Inferences: A Developmental Study." *Journal of Personality and Social Psychology,* 1986, *50,* 889–898.

Biernat, M. "Gender Stereotypes and the Relationship Between Masculinity and Femininity: A Developmental Analysis." *Journal of Personality and Social Psychology,* 1991, *61,* 351–365.

Boston, M. B., and Levy, G. D. "Changes and Differences in Preschoolers' Understanding of Gender Scripts." *Cognitive Development,* 1991, *6,* 417–432.

Bukowski, W. H., Gauze, C., Hoza, B., and Newcomb, A. F. "Differences and Consistency Between Same-Sex and Other-Sex Peer Relationships During Early Adolescence." *Developmental Psychology,* 1993, *29,* 255–263.

Bussey, K., and Bandura, A. "Self-Regulatory Mechanisms Governing Gender Development." *Child Development,* 1992, *63,* 1236–1250.

Carter, D. B. "The Roles of Peers in Sex Role Socialization." In D. B. Carter (ed.), *Current Conceptions of Sex Roles and Sex Typing: Theory and Research.* New York: Praeger, 1987.

Carter, D. B., and McCloskey, L. A. "Peers and the Maintenance of Sex-Typed Behavior: The Development of Children's Conceptions of Cross-Gender Behavior in Their Peers." *Social Cognition,* 1984, *2,* 294–314.

Charlesworth, W. R., and Hartup, W. W. "Positive Social Reinforcement in the Nursery School Peer Group." *Child Development,* 1967, *38,* 993–1002.

Charlesworth, W. R., and LaFreniere, P. "Dominance, Friendship Utilization and Resource Utilization in Preschool Children's Groups." *Ethology and Sociobiology,* 1983, *4,* 175–186.

Deaux, K., and Lewis, L. L. "Structure of Gender Stereotypes: Interrelationships Among Components and Gender Label." *Journal of Personality and Social Psychology,* 1984, *46,* 991–1004.

Deaux, K., and Major, B. "Putting Gender into Context: An Interactive Model of Gender-Related Behavior." *Psychological Review,* 1987, *94,* 369–389.

Devine, P. G. "Stereotypes and Prejudice: Their Automatic and Controlled Components." *Journal of Personality and Social Psychology,* 1989, *56,* 5–18.

Duveen, G., and Lloyd, B. "The Significance of Social Identities." *British Journal of Social Psychology,* 1986, *65,* 325–340.

Ellis, S., Rogoff, B., and Cromer, C. "Research Reports: Age Segregation in Children's Social Interactions." *Developmental Psychology,* 1981, *17,* 399–407.

Fagot, B. I. "Changes in Thinking About Early Sex Role Development." *Developmental Review,* 1985, *5,* 83–98.

Fagot, B. I., Leinbach, M. D., and Hagan, R. "Gender Labeling and the Adoption of Sex-Typed Behaviors." *Developmental Psychology,* 1986, *22,* 440–443.

Goodenough, F. *Developmental Psychology: An Introduction to the Study of Human Behavior.* New York: Appleton-Century, 1934.

Hartup, W. W. "Peer Relations." In P. H. Mussen (ed.), *Handbook of Child Psychology.* (4th ed.) Vol. 4: *Socialization, Personality, and Social Development.* (E. M. Hetherington, vol. ed.) New York: Wiley, 1983.

Huston, A. C. "Sex-typing." In P. H. Mussen (ed.), *Handbook of Child Psychology.* (4th ed.) Vol. 4: *Socialization, Personality, and Social Development.* (E. M. Hetherington, vol. ed.) New York: Wiley, 1983.

Huston, A. C. "The Development of Sex Typing: Themes from Recent Research." *Developmental Review,* 1985, *5,* 1–17.

Jacklin, C. N., and Maccoby, E. E. "Social Behavior at 33 Months in Same-Sex and Mixed-Sex Dyads." *Child Development,* 1978, *49,* 557–569.

Kuhn, D., Nash, S. C., and Brucken, L. "Sex Role Concepts of Two- and Three-Year-Old Children." *Child Development,* 1978, *49,* 445–451.

LaFreniere, P., and Charlesworth, W. R. "Preschool Peer Status, Behavior and Resource Utilization in a Cooperative/Competitive Situation." *International Journal of Behavioral Development,* 1987, *10,* 345–358.

LaFreniere, P., Strayer, F. F., and Gauthier, R. "The Emergence of Same-Sex Preferences Among Preschool Peers: A Developmental Ethological Perspective." *Child Development,* 1984, *55,* 1958–1965.

Langlois, J. H., Gottfried, N. W., and Seay, B. "The Influence of Sex of Peer on the Social Behavior of Preschool Children." *Developmental Psychology,* 1973, *8,* 93–98.

Leahy, R. L., and Shirk, S. R. "The Development of Classificatory Skills and Sex-Trait Stereotypes in Young Children." *Sex Roles,* 1984, *10,* 281–292.

Leaper, C. "Influence and Involvement in Children's Discourse: Age, Gender, and Partner Effects." *Child Development,* 1991, *62,* 797–811.

Leinbach, M. D., and Fagot, B. I. "Categorical Habituation to Male and Female Faces: Gender-Schematic Processing in Infancy." *Infant Behavior and Development,* 1993, *16,* 317–332.

Levy, G. D. "Relations Among Aspects of Children's Social Environments, Gender Schematization, Gender Role Knowledge, and Flexibility." *Sex Roles,* 1989, *21,* 803–823.

Levy, G. D., and Barth, J. M. "Behavioral and Cognitive Facets of Early Gender-Role Development: Bridging the Gap." Paper presented at the Conference on Human Development, Richmond, Va., Mar. 1990.

Levy, G. D., and Fivush, R. "Scripts and Gender: A New Approach for Examining Gender Role Development." *Developmental Review,* 1993, *13,* 126–146.

Maccoby, E. E. "Gender as a Social Category." *Developmental Psychology,* 1988, *24,* 755–765.

Maccoby, E. E. "Gender and Relationships: A Developmental Account." *American Psychologist,* 1990, *45,* 513–520.

Maccoby, E. E., and Jacklin, C. N. "Gender Segregation in Childhood." In H. Reese (ed.), *Advances in Child Development and Behavior.* Vol. 20. San Diego: Academic Press, 1987.

Markus, H., Crane, M., Bernstein, S., and Siladi, M. "Self-Schemas and Gender." *Journal of Personality and Social Psychology,* 1982, *42,* 38–50.

Martin, C. L. "Beyond Knowledge-Based Conceptions of Schematic Processing." Paper presented at the meeting of the Society for Research in Child Development, Kansas City, Mo., Apr. 1989a.

Martin, C. L. "Children's Use of Gender-Related Information in Making Social Judgments." *Developmental Psychology,* 1989b, *25,* 80–88.

Martin, C. L. "The Role of Cognition in Understanding Gender Effects." In H. Reese (ed.), *Advances in Child Development and Behavior.* Vol. 23. San Diego: Academic Press, 1991.

Martin, C. L. "New Directions for Investigating Children's Gender Knowledge." *Developmental Review,* 1993, *13,* 184–204.

Martin, C. L., Eisenbud, L., and Rose, H. A. "The Influence of Explicit and Implicit Gender Knowledge on Children's Social Judgments." Under review.

Martin, C. L., and Halverson, C. F., Jr. "A Schematic Processing Model of Sex Typing and Stereotyping in Children." *Child Development,* 1981, *54,* 563–574.

Martin, C. L., and Halverson, C. F., Jr. "The Roles of Cognition in Sex Role Acquisition." In D. B. Carter (ed.), *Current Conceptions of Sex Roles and Sex Typing: Theory and Research.* New York: Praeger, 1987.

Martin, C. L., Wood, C. H., and Little, J. K. "The Development of Gender Stereotype Components. *Child Development,* 1990, *61,* 1891–1904.

Medin, D. L. "Concepts and Conceptual Structure." *American Psychologist,* 1989, *44,* 1469–1481.

Poulin-Dubois, D., Serbin, L. A., Kenyon, B., and Derbyshire, A. "Infants' Intermodal Knowledge About Gender." Unpublished manuscript, 1992.

Powlishta, K. K., and Maccoby, E. E. "Resource Utilization in Mixed-Sex Dyads: The Influence of Adult Presence and Task Type." *Sex Roles,* 1990, *23,* 223–240.

Rubin, Z. *Children's Friendships.* Huntington, N.Y.: Fontana Press, 1980.

Serbin, L. A., Powlishta, K. K., and Gulko, J. "The Development of Sex Typing in Middle Childhood." *Monographs of the Society for Research in Child Development,* 1993, *58* (2, Serial 232).

Serbin, L. A., and Sprafkin, C. "The Salience of Gender and the Process of Sex Typing in Three- to Seven-Year-Old Children." *Child Development,* 1986, *57,* 1188–1199.

Serbin, L. A., Sprafkin, C., Elman, M., and Doyle, A. B. "The Early Development of Sex Differentiated Patterns of Social Influence." *Canadian Journal of Social Science,* 1982, *14* (4), 350–363.

Serbin, L. A., Tonick, I. V., and Sternglanz, S. "Shaping Cooperative Cross-Sex Play." *Child Development,* 1977, *48,* 924–929.

Signorella, M. L., Bigler, R. S., and Liben, L. S. "Developmental Differences in Children's Gender Schemata About Others: A Meta-Analytic Review." *Developmental Review,* 1993, *13,* 147–183.

Stoddard, T., and Turiel, E. "Children's Concepts of Cross-Gender Activities." *Child Development,* 1985, *56,* 1241–1252.

Stoneman, Z., Brody, G. H., and MacKinnon, C. "Naturalistic Observations of Children's Activities and Roles While Playing with Their Siblings and Friends. *Child Development,* 1984, *55,* 617–627.

Tajfel, H. *Human Groups and Social Categories.* Cambridge, England: Cambridge University Press, 1981.

Thorne, B. "Girls and Boys Together, but Mostly Apart." In W. W. Hartup and Z. Rubin (eds.), *Relationship and Development.* Hillsdale, N.J.: Erlbaum, 1986.

Wilder, D., and Allen, W. "Effects of Social Categorization and Belief Similarity upon Intergroup Behavior." *Personality and Social Psychology Bulletin,* 1974, *1,* 281–283.

CAROL LYNN MARTIN is associate professor in the Department of Family Resources and Human Development at Arizona State University, Tempe.

Past research and new longitudinal data examine the relationship between children's peer relations and the development of social and cognitive competence.

Peer Relations and the Development of Competence in Boys and Girls

Beverly I. Fagot

By the time they are three years old, boys and girls around the world participate in different activities and show different behavioral styles (Whiting and Edwards, 1988), play more with same-sex peers, and avoid opposite-sex peers (Maccoby, 1988). Different cultures have very different ideas about the capabilities of the young child, and in many cultures, preschool children are not considered capable of learning through instruction (Whiting and Edwards, 1988). In such cultures, children are often taught their social roles through guided participation within ongoing family social groups (Rogoff, 1990) rather than formal school settings. As documented by Whiting and Edwards (1988), there are cultures in which the family segregates young boys and girls from a very early age. (Also, Goodall, 1986, notes that young chimpanzee females are kept much closer to the mother and are not allowed to join the free roaming playgroups of males. Female chimp friendships are more closely tied to family groups, and the females play in smaller groups than do the males.) However, in Western Europe, there is little family pressure for sex segregation of young children, yet in nursery schools, which often promote a lack of sex segregation, researchers have long noted that much of the children's play is in same-sex groups. Charlesworth and Hartup (1967) were among the first to document this phenomenon. Fagot and Patterson (1969) and Fagot (1977) showed that boys who attempted to play in groups of girls or in activities

The research reported in this chapter was supported by grant HM 37911 from the Behavioral Sciences Research Branch, Family Processes Division, National Institute of Mental Health, and grant HD 19739 from the Center for Research for Mothers and Children, National Institute of Child and Human Development (NICHD).

favored by girls received a good deal more peer criticism than other boys. In addition, such criticism continued even when the boys then attempted to play in typical male activities. Fagot (1985) showed that girls received more positive feedback when playing with other girls but that it was all right for girls to play in male activities. Boys, on the other hand, received positive feedback only when engaged with other boys and when engaged in male activities. Serbin, Connor, and Citron (1981) have shown that it is very difficult to change the pattern of boys' play through teacher intervention but relatively easy to change girls' play.

In the preschool classroom, therefore, gender segregation exists, and boys and girls may already be spending a good portion of their time in different activities. Sex differences in toy and activity preference among preschool children have been documented in different cultures (O'Brien and Huston, 1985; Smith and Connolly, 1980; Trautner, Helbing, and Sahm, 1985). Similar differences in behavioral styles have been noted by observers in several different cultures and in nonhuman primates (Blurton-Jones, 1967; DePietro, 1981). In particular, young males engage in more rough-and-tumble play, even though there are minimal sex differences in large motor activity.

An important consistent difference between boys and girls in preschools is that boys engage in more physical aggression (Maccoby and Jacklin, 1974). Even for young children, the male stereotype is heavily defined by aggressive props and activities. In attempting to develop a list of very stereotyped activities or props among four-year-olds, Hort (1989) found that five of the six most masculine items (for example, guns, knives, and fighting) involved aggression. While these results might seem to suggest that preschools encourage the development of sex-differentiated behaviors, this may not be entirely true. Organized preschools place boys and girls in closer contact than they would otherwise be; in some cultures, it is only within such a setting that boys and girls play together at all (Whiting and Edwards, 1988).

Several theories have emerged to account for children's tendency to sort into gender-segregated playgroups. LaFreniere, Strayer, and Gauthier (1984) built upon the behavioral compatibility hypothesis (Goodenough, 1934), which suggests that children play in sex-segregated groups because of different interests and behavioral styles. Maccoby (1988) reported the differences in participation in rough-and-tumble play. Serbin, Moller, Powlishta, Gulko, and Colburne (see Chapter One) found that play in same-sex groups was more cooperative than in mixed-sex groups, that more socially skilled children chose to play with other socially skilled children regardless of sex, and that, within same-sex groups, girls were more socially skilled than boys. They suggested that gender segregation is related to different behavioral styles but not to specific toy and activity preferences. In a cross-sectional sample, two colleagues and I (Fagot, Leinbach, and Hagan, 1986) found that knowledge of gender labels was related to gender segregation. This study was done with slightly younger children (twenty-one to forty months of age) than previous studies, and it suggested that children's ability to label both themselves and other children might accelerate the pace of sex-stereotyping. I replicated this finding with a longitudinal sample (Fagot, 1990). In addition, I found that eighteen-month-old children showed a consistent preference for playing either with adults or with other children. Children who preferred play with adults played more in mixed-sex groups, while children who preferred play with other children played in gender-segregated groups. Differences in behavioral style at eighteen months promoted differences in the composition of the groups children played in a year later, at thirty months.

Gender segregation very likely occurs because of a number of factors. Children who are in the process of developing gender schemas use every cue available to adopt the appropriate behaviors. (Playing with those like yourself is a powerful indicator that you are, indeed, a boy or a girl.) Children also sort themselves in terms of behavioral compatibility. I found (Fagot, 1985) that preschool children respond to and change their behaviors at the instigation of their own sex but not at the instigation of the opposite sex.

Maccoby (1988) stated that the first step toward knowing what it means to be male or female consists of self-labeling, an ability unlikely to be secure before the age of two. Such a statement reflects the cognitive-developmental view that young children construct their knowledge of the world at the level their mental capabilities permit, a view that places the acquisition of sex-typed behaviors and attitudes subsequent to the desire to act in accord with one's self-perceived identity as a boy or girl. However, in emphasizing attainment of successively higher levels of reasoning, cognitive-developmental theory appears to overestimate the degree of understanding children must possess before knowledge of sex-typing can be shown and can begin to affect behavior (Carter, 1987; Leinbach and Fagot, 1986; Levy and Fivush, 1993; Martin, 1993). Tests of gender knowledge have been constructed to ensure that achievement of a particular level is not credited unless a correct judgment of a target child's sex can be held fast in the face of perceptual transformation of the stimulus (Emmerich, Goldman, Kirsh, and Sharabany, 1977) or repeated questioning (Slaby and Frey, 1975). Such stringent criteria have tended to mask early knowledge and to leave children under three looking curiously incompetent with regard to gender.

A Recent Longitudinal Study

There are very few data reported on measures across settings, agents, and time for young children. I and my colleagues at the University of Oregon Psychology Department Child Laboratory have been following a group of 156 children from eighteen months to seven years of age. We have seen these children with their parents at eighteen months, thirty months, and four, five, and seven years of age. In addition, from eighteen to thirty months of age, the children were observed in playgroups. Teachers rated the children in the playgroups, and at ages five, six, and seven. We have been very interested in examining the correlates of gender-role development, including the development of preferences for same-sex peers, as the children enter each new developmental stage. From observations in the peer playgroups, we found that children who had engaged in negative interactions with their parents at eighteen months also engaged in negative interactions with peers in the playgroups. However, those negative interactions correlated quite differently for boys and girls with peer ratings from teachers, self, and mothers as the children grew older. Boys who received high levels of negatives from other boys in playgroups rated themselves at age four as more accepted by peers, although mothers rated them as having difficulty with peers. Teacher ratings did not correlate with any other measures for boys. Negative reactions from girls did not relate to self-ratings or to mother ratings of peer problems. Girls who received high levels of negatives from playgroup peers, either boys or girls, rated themselves as less accepted by peers. Mothers rated girls who received negatives from female peers as having more difficulty with peers, and there was a trend for teachers to see these same girls as having more difficulty. Mothers and teachers did not agree at all on which boys were having difficulty with peers, but they did show a low but significant level of agreement on which girls were having difficulty with peers.

Peer relationships obviously play an extremely important role in the child's social development and long-term adjustment. There is an extensive research literature on peer networks and the consequences for individual children's positions in a network. However, it is equally important to understand the child's own feelings concerning his or her friends and their acceptance of him or her. In addition, the social interaction of children with their friends is an informative, though understudied, measure of the quality of the friendship. In our longitudinal study, we examined the relation between early ratings of attachment to the mother at eighteen months and peer relations at age seven.

Attachment theory assumes that children develop an internal working model of relationships with their first attachment; therefore, the quality of this first attachment should be related to the quality of other relationships, including those with peers. While there have been few sex differences reported for attachment classifications, there are beginning to be reports of sex-differentiated reactions by peers and teachers, which may be related to gender segregation. Turner (1991), using the Cassidy and Marvin (1990) preschool measure of attachment, found that boys who were insecure were more aggressive and disruptive than secure children but insecure girls were more dependent than secure children. With the same group of children, Turner (1993) also found that insecure children directed more dependency requests toward teachers. Insecure boys' requests were ignored, whereas insecure girls were given more help than secure children. It is becoming clear that boys and girls may receive very different reactions from their environment even when they share relationship styles. If these findings hold for other studies, we may find a consistent sex-by-attachment classification, which would predict boys moving into more active, rough-and-tumble play, while girls move to quieter, more teacher-oriented play. At this point, we can say only that it is possible that a child's attachment classification influences the degree of gender segregation.

Children in our longitudinal study took part in the Strange Situation procedure at eighteen months of age and were classified according to the

Ainsworth attachment categories (Ainsworth, Blehar, Waters, and Wall, 1978). We then examined the children's own perceptions of their peer relations, as well as their understanding of friendships, at age seven, in relation to their attachment classifications at eighteen months. The children had filled out the Pictorial Scale of Perceived Competence and Social Acceptance for Young Children (Harter and Pike, 1984), which includes a scale of peer acceptance. Boys who had been classified as insecure (both avoidant and resistant) rated themselves as more accepted by peers than secure boys and all girls; whereas girls who had been rated as avoidant rated themselves as less accepted. We can only speculate about the reasons behind these differences, but it should be noted that peer-rejected boys were very poor at rating their actual standing within groups. We also examined the relation between attachment classification and the children's ability to describe friendships on the Friendship Interview (Damon, 1977). There were no differences in level of friendship ratings on the Damon Friendship Interview by attachment classification. However, children's ratings of their own friends on this interview were related to attachment classification, with insecure children describing their friends in less positive terms.

We also examined behavioral interactions in three laboratory tasks in which the longitudinal subject child was interacting with a peer. One task was a competitive game, and another was a cooperative activity in which the children made a mask together. There were no sex differences in positive and negative interaction in either the cooperative or the competitive task. Children who had been classified as insecure had fewer negative interactions in the competitive task but showed no differences in the cooperative task. There were no significant differences in ratings of children by experimenters or coders in terms of sex or attachment classification. Both the coder and experimenter impressions were highly correlated with the amount of negative behaviors seen in the interactions, indicating that they were valid measures of interactive style. We also examined children's behavior in a free play task. In this task, insecure children showed more awkward and anxious behaviors than secure children.

Parents did not see differences among the attachment groups or by sex either in peer relations or behavior problems, but there were significant sex differences in teacher ratings. On the Walker-McConnell Scale of Social Competence and School Adjustment (Walker and McConnell, 1988), teachers saw girls as less well liked by peers than boys, but they saw boys as having more negative interactions with peers than girls. Teachers rated children with insecure attachments as being more negative with peers. While there were no gender effects at age seven in grade school teachers' reactions to the children, Fagot and Kavanagh (1990) found that preschool teachers rated girls who had been classified as avoidant as being more difficult to deal with and having more trouble with peers than secure girls. In effect, avoidant girls in preschool tended to play with objects and by themselves more than secure girls, so in that way they were not as sex-typed. Since this effect was not reported at age seven by grade school teachers, it may be an age-specific finding seen only in the preschool setting.

Implications for Cognitive Development

Gender segregation and the resulting differences in activity choice have implications for cognitive skills. Block (1983), using Piaget's mechanism of adaptation, suggested that young boys engage in activities that require them to change their own structures. She suggested that boys' toys and activities allow them to solve problems in new and creative ways but that girls were more likely to engage in activities that imitated life roles and that did not require them to change but allowed them to rehearse these cultural roles; therefore, girls might actually know more about the expectations of the culture. Block (1983) suggested that these differences in early play styles lead to differences in intellectual and emotional development. Girls utilize existing cognitive and social structures that are modified by incremental steps. They are given toys that encourage the learning of rules and imitation of behaviors and are encouraged by adults to keep in close contact. Boys are given toys that force them to develop their own schemas and to find out how the toys work. Boys are also encouraged to engage more in activities with peers and not with adults. Block hypothesized that, as a consequence of these differences in play styles and in interactions with adults and peers, girls' development is more stable than boys', because girls can draw upon adults for help while boys do not use adult help as effectively but are forced to restructure more often and to produce their own unique solutions.

Are there data to support Block's hypothesis? For the past fifteen years in the University of Oregon Psychology Department Child Laboratory, my colleagues and I have been studying just this question. Are there differences that can be documented in play styles of boys and girls from one to five years of age? How do such differences relate to the children's own construction of gender schemas as well as to the reactions of others to the children? Do the reactions of teachers and peers help initiate the differences in boys' and girls' play styles, or does the child's own emerging construction of gender precede such differences? Finally, is there any indication that such differences in play styles have the kind of long-term consequences for social and emotional development predicted by Block?

The first question is the simplest to answer. Yes, there are differences in the play styles of boys and girls, and the differences have not really changed over the last twenty years. Girls engage in more doll play and domestic rehearsal, more art activities and dressing up. Boys play more with transportation toys, blocks, and carpentry toys. Boys also engage in more aggressive activities and play more in larger peer groups. Girls spend more time talking and spend far more time with teachers than do boys (Fagot, 1984c; Fagot and Patterson, 1969). As they grow older, both boys and girls increasingly spend more time in same-sex playgroups and actively avoid the opposite sex (Fagot, 1985; Fagot and Patterson, 1969).

When do sex differences in play styles begin to appear? In our laboratory, we do not see differences in play styles in twelve- to eighteen-month-old boys and girls, either in terms of toy choices or interactive styles. When a group of children twelve to fourteen months of age was observed for three months in infant playgroups, two styles of interaction were recorded: assertive behaviors (hitting, pushing, shoving, grabbing for another's toys) and communicative behaviors (gesturing, babbling, or talking). There were no differences in the occurrences of these behaviors between boys and girls. The adult caretaker's reactions to the child's initiations, however, was highly dependent upon the sex of the child. If a boy produced an assertive behavior, he received a response from the teacher 41 percent of the time, but if a girl produced the same behavior, she received a response from the teacher only 10 percent of the time. If a girl produced a positive type of communicative behavior, she received a response from the teacher 65 percent of the time, while a boy initiating the same behavior received a response 48 percent of the time. On the other hand, boys who demanded attention negatively by whining, crying, screaming, or by pulling at the teacher received attention 55 percent of the time, while girls performing similar acts received a response only 18 percent of the time. When we looked at these same children approximately one year later, we found sex differences in the children's behavior. Boys performed more aggressive acts, while girls spent more time talking and interacting with the teachers (Fagot, Hagan, Leinbach, and Kronsberg, 1985). We found that sex differences in play styles and in interactive styles began to appear from twenty to twenty-four months of age and were well established by the time the children were thirty-six months old.

In a study with slightly older children, I found (Fagot, 1985) that girls changed their behaviors when either teachers or other girls reacted to them, while boys reacted only to the responses of other boys. In addition, girls' peer groups tolerated play with many more play materials than did boys'. Boys' peer groups responded negatively to boys who played with "girls' toys" and to boys who played with girls, so that boys were being given constant feedback on both appropriate play styles and appropriate playmates. Girls were given feedback on appropriate playmates only. When we combine this with the tendency of boys to ignore teacher feedback and to spend much less time interacting with teachers than girls do, we start to see that, indeed, the same playgroup or preschool environment does not provide boys and girls with the same socialization experiences.

Finally, is there any support for Block's ideas that differences in intellectual and emotional development arise from these early differences in play and interactional styles? So far, such data are only correlational. We know that boys lag behind girls in their ability to deal with school-like tasks and that they show more emotional problems during early childhood. Also, boys who show extreme aggressiveness and girls who show extreme dependency as two-year-olds continue to have the same problems for as long as two additional years (Fagot, 1984a, 1984b). The relation to intellectual development is less well documented, but girls who show extreme feminine play preferences are less likely to do well in math and science (Fagot and Littman, 1975).

There is also evidence concerning children's cross-sex interactions. Here, there is a noticeable difference in the reactions of the peer group to each gender. Girls who attempt to join male peer groups and participate in cross-sex behaviors are, at worst, ignored (Fagot, 1977; Maccoby, 1988). Boys who attempt to participate in feminine behaviors receive more negative feedback from peers, both boys and girls (Fagot 1977, 1989). In a German sample, Trautner, Helbing, and Sahm (1985) reported that boys did not value female activities and disliked boys who did, whereas girls did value female activities but did not react negatively when other girls tried out male activities.

Gender differences in preschool are not confined to play with different toys in gender-segregated groups. Girls spend a great deal more time with their teachers (Fagot and Patterson, 1969; Serbin, O'Leary, Kent, and Tonick, 1973), and consequently, teachers interact more with girls. Girls also respond more to teachers' directions (Fagot, 1985; Serbin, Connor, and Citron, 1981) and avail themselves more of teachers' consolations (Feldbaum, Christenson, and O'Neal, 1980). Teachers tend to react to children when they are engaged in table play, particularly art and school-like behaviors (Fagot and Patterson, 1969). There has been some concern that preschool might feminize boys (Sexton, 1968), but extensive further studies have suggested that this is a misreading of the literature (Vroegh, 1976).

Fagot (1981) found that girls clustered around both male and female teachers, while boys more often played around the edges of classrooms. This effect was stronger when teachers were experienced than when they were inexperienced. Lee and Kedar-Voivodas (1977) found that preschool teachers interacted more with children who took a pupil role than with children playing in other activities. Pupil-role behaviors overlap more with female-preferred behaviors (for example, many kinds of table games) than with male-preferred behaviors (for example, large motor activities). Moreover, teachers fail to react to either boys or girls involved in traditional sex-typed behaviors (for example, rough-and-tumble play or doll play).

Differences in boys' and girls' preferences for highly structured versus less structured activities influence more than gender-role development. Carpenter and Huston (1980) found that children of either sex who preferred highly structured activities were more compliant and used toys in less novel ways. In contrast, children who preferred less structure tended to interact more with peers. Because more boys than girls took part in the less structured activities, boys were more likely to interact with other boys. Gender segregation may therefore be encouraged by these sex differences in activity preference.

Carpenter (1983) suggested that long-term and continued participation in either less or more structured activities teaches different styles of interaction with the environment. Highly structured activities contribute to the learning of rules and the accommodation of the child to the environment, while less structured activities may force children to adapt in new ways to the environment. Block (1983), as described, took this beyond preschool and suggested that, in general, girls are taught to accommodate to rules while boys are forced to adapt to a lack of rules. Maccoby (1988) noted that girls prefer the protection that teachers provide from boys and that girls' flocking toward the teacher may be more an avoidance of boys than a preference for the teacher. It should be noted that children who prefer greater structure are learning the rules of schooling, and this preference for higher structure may be one reason that girls outperform boys in early school years. Additionally, high structure has been found to inhibit both aggression and rough-and-tumble play, but this does not appear to be an indication that children—boys in particular—are learning self-control: in unstructured situations, these children remain aggressive and boisterous (Smith and Connolly, 1980).

We do believe that toddlers and preschool children are very motivated to behave in ways they perceive as defining their own sex. Gender identity is a very important construct, and children who fail to develop an appropriate identity are in trouble (Zucker; 1985, Zucker and Green, 1992). Children will try to match their play behaviors to those of other children of the same sex and will congregate in areas that have toys obviously sex-stereotyped for their own sex. While teachers can reinforce children to increase the frequency of cross-sex play, they will not have much success forcing preschool children to behave in other-sex ways over the long run (Serbin, Connor, and Iler, 1979; Serbin, Tonick, and Sternglanz, 1977). At this stage, the child's goal of establishing a stable gender identity will conflict with such attempts. However, styles of play actually have little to do with sex-stereotyping, and the wise teacher can encourage a broad play repertoire that will allow children to engage in different types of play, without trying to force them to engage in other-sex play.

For example, many believe that both boys and girls should engage in some type of large motor play to increase coordination. We find no differences between boys and girls in large motor play until two and one-half years of age. When we looked at our data carefully, we found that this difference was due to girls' insisting on wearing dresses to school, often accompanied by slippery shoes. Now, it is quite reasonable for a teacher to tell parents that, for the sake of safety, all children must wear shoes with rubber soles and that children should wear clothes that allow them to engage in running, jumping, and dancing. We find that parents are quite happy with this and that girls will not complain if told that school rules forbid long dresses and slippery shoes. When this simple step is taken, boys and girls again engage equally in large motor play.

As another example, very often we find a difference in the amount of block play engaged in by boys and girls. We believe that the skills learned through block play are an important component of a child's cognitive development. However, if you examine the block corner in many preschools, you find that blocks are kept with transportation toys and that such corners contain many boys and no girls. Simply separating blocks and transportation toys increases the number of girls playing with blocks. While these girls often build houses rather than forts, they still learn spatial skills, Concentrating upon the play skill to be acquired rather than play content allows the teacher to make slight changes that allow both boys and girls to use this very important set of skills.

If Block is correct that different styles of play, which are related to sex-typing but not necessarily tied to any definition of the sexes, influence intellectual development, then it behooves those who work with young children to examine environments carefully to ensure that they are not closing children out of important skills through classroom organization. However, intellectual development is not the only area in which sex-stereotyping is felt to affect development. If children spend a large amount of time playing in single-sex groups and developing only one style of interaction, might this be a problem at adolescence?

Implications for Development of Intimacy

One concern with gender segregation throughout childhood is that boys and girls will meet in adolescence virtually as strangers, having learned different styles of interaction and different coping styles (see also Chapter Five). Certainly my own longitudinal study suggests that boys and girls interpret the same pattern of interactions in very different ways. Gottman (1994) points out that sociometric and observational data do not tell the entire story here, for indeed cross-sex friendships exist throughout childhood. However, after preschool, they are hidden from the peer group at large, tending to take place within the confines of children's homes and/or neighborhoods. Gottman reports that males' cross-sex friendships tend to be very intense emotional relationships and that while males' same-sex friendships can be used to work through difficulties, there is a different quality to discussions when a girl is present. Boy pairs appear to use mastery mediated through fantasy or humor to deal with fears, whereas, with a girl present, there is increased use of emotional support mediated through comfort, soothing, and love to combat fear. Gottman points out that girl pairs do not seem to discuss fear as much, in part because it is most often a boy who introduces the fearful topic. When girls do discuss fears together, they use reassurance to comfort each other. We see then that, for some children, childhood is not as gender-segregated as it appears from surveys of school data. Yet we really do not know if children who have cross-sex friendships are more able to interact with the opposite sex throughout life. Given that we see, even as early as preschool, boys discounting the attempts of girls to interact with them and female teachers to control them (Fagot, 1985), this is an area of concern that needs additional study.

Conclusion

At this point there appears to be a great deal of evidence for the self-perpetuating nature of gender segregation. Such segregation appears to be initiated and maintained within the peer group (LaFreniere, Strayer, and Gauthier, 1984). It appears that girls may first begin the segregation, but by age four, boys are highly active in maintaining differences. Within this segregated world, boys and girls practice different skills. For young boys, this segregated world appears to have some negative consequences, as they do not relate as often to adults, and throughout childhood, they continue to have more difficulty than girls in interactions with teachers. In addition, many of the activities boys engage in do not lead to school skills, and they appear to begin school with lower skills than do girls. In addition, boys' peer groups have less supervision and are more likely to engage in behaviors unacceptable to the adult world. Boys then show a much higher level of oppositional and defiant behaviors. Finally, all-boy groups appear to attempt to problem solve through mastery, dominance, or humor and often fail to use other techniques. As young children, girls appear to fare better in the gender-segregated world. They learn to take direction from adults and use it very effectively to problem solve. Girls also rehearse school skills in the early years and are better prepared for school. In addition, female peer groups appear to use a large variety of problem-solving skills. However, gender segregation may well affect girls negatively as they get older. First, by not emphasizing mastery skills, they may find themselves at a disadvantage in direct confrontations with males. It is also possible that certain types of skills are not learned with the usual play activities of girls (for examples, spatial abilities or the ability to break set patterns). However, despite strong peer-group pressure, some children maintain cross-sex friendships throughout childhood. Undoubtedly, the lives of most children include a broader repertoire of behaviors than we see.

References

Ainsworth, M.D.S., Blehar, M. C., Waters, E., and Wall, S. *Patterns of Attachment: A Psychological Study of the Strange Situation.* Hillsdale, N.J.: Erlbaum, 1978.

Block, J. H. "Differential Premises Arising from Differential Socialization of the Sexes: Some Conjectures." *Child Development,* 1983, *54,* 1335–1354.

Blurton-Jones, N. G. "An Ethological Study of Some Aspects of Social Behaviour of Children in Nursery School." In E. D. Morris (ed.), *Primate Ethology.* London: Weidenfeld & Nicolson, 1967.

Carpenter, C. J. "Activity Structure and Play: Implications for Socialization." In M. B. Liss (ed.), *Social and Cognitive Skills: Sex Roles and Children's Play.* San Diego: Academic Press, 1983.

Carpenter, C. J., and Huston, A. J. "Activity Structure and Sex-Typed Behavior in Preschool Children." *Child Development,* 1980, *51,* 862–872.

Carter, D. B. "Sex Role Research and the Future: New Directions for Research." In D. B. Carter (ed.), *Current Conceptions of Sex Roles and Sex Typing: Theory and Research.* New York: Praeger, 1987.

Cassidy, J., and Marvin, R. *Attachment Organization in Preschool Children: Coding Guidelines.* Seattle: MacArthur Working Group on Attachment, 1990.

Charlesworth, R., and Hartup, W. W. "Positive Social Reinforcement in the Nursery School Peer Group." *Child Development,* 1967, *38,* 315–320.

Damon, W. *The Social World of the Child.* San Francisco: Jossey-Bass, 1977.

DiPietro, J. "Rough and Tumble Play: A Function of Gender." *Developmental Psychology,* 1981, *17,* 50–58.

Emmerich, W., Goldman, K., Kirsh, B., and Sharabany, R. "Evidence for a Transitional Phase in the Development of Gender Constancy." *Child Development,* 1977, *48,* 930–936.

Fagot, B. I. "Consequences of Moderate Cross-Gender Behavior in Preschool Children." *Child Development,* 1977, *48,* 902–907.

Fagot, B. I. "Male and Female Teachers: Do They Treat Boys and Girls Differently?" *Sex Roles,* 1981, *7,* 263–271.

Fagot, B. I. "The Child's Expectations of Differences in Adult Male and Female Interactions." *Sex Roles,* 1984a, *11,* 593–600.

Fagot, B. I. "The Consequences of Problem Behavior in Toddler Children." *Journal of Abnormal Child Psychology,* 1984b, *12,* 385–395.

Fagot, B. I. "Teacher and Peer Reactions to Boys' and Girls' Play Styles." *Sex Roles,* 1984c, *11,* 691–702.

Fagot, B. I. "Beyond the Reinforcement Principle: Another Step Toward Understanding Sex Roles." *Developmental Psychology,* 1985, *21,* 1097–1104.

Fagot, B. I. "Cross-Gender Behavior and Its Consequences for Boys." *Italian Journal of Clinical and Cultural Psychology,* 1989, *1,* 79–84.

Fagot, B. I. "A Longitudinal Study of Gender Segregation: Infancy to Preschool." Symposium presented at the International Conference on Infancy Studies, Montreal, 1990.

Fagot, B. I., Hagan, R., Leinbach, M. D., and Kronsberg, S. "Differential Reactions to Assertive and Communicative Acts of Toddler Boys and Girls." *Child Development,* 1985, *56,* 1499–1505.

Fagot, B. I., and Kavanagh, K. "The Prediction of Antisocial Behaviors from Avoidant Attachment Classification." *Child Development,* 1990, *61,* 864–873.

Fagot, B. I., Leinbach, M. D., and Hagan, R. "Gender Labeling and the Adoption of Sextyped Behaviors." *Developmental Psychology,* 1986, *22,* 220–443.

Fagot, B. I., and Littman, I. "Stability of Sex Role and Play Interests from Preschool to Elementary School." *Journal of Psychology,* 1975, *89,* 285–292.

Fagot, B. I., and Patterson, G. R. "An in Vivo Analysis of Reinforcing Contingencies for Sex-Role Behaviors in the Preschool Child." *Developmental Psychology,* 1969, *1,* 563–568.

Feldbaum, C. L., Christenson, T. E., and O'Neal, E. C. "An Observational Study of the Assimilation of the Newcomer to the Preschool." *Child Development,* 1980, *51,* 497–507.

Goodall, J. *The Chimpanzees of Gombe: Patterns of Behavior.* Cambridge, Mass.: Harvard University Press, 1986.

Goodenough, F. *Developmental Psychology: An Introduction to the Study of Human Behavior.* New York: Appleton-Century, 1934.

Gottman, J. M. "Why Can't Men and Women Get Along?" In D. Canary and L. Stafford (eds.), *Communication and Relational Maintenance.* San Diego: Academic Press, 1994.

Harter, S., and Pike, R. "The Pictorial Scale of Perceived Competence and Social Acceptance for Young Children." *Child Development,* 1984, *55,* 1962–1982.

Hort, B. "Jane's Gun and John's Mascara: A Difference in Peer Reactions to Males and Females Who Display Cross-Gender Behaviors." Unpublished doctoral dissertation, Department of Psychology, University of Oregon, 1989.

LaFreniere, P., Strayer, F. F., and Gauthier, R. "The Emergence of Same-Sex Affiliative Preferences Among Preschool Peers: A Developmental/Ethological Perspective." *Child Development,* 1984, *55,* 1958–1965.

Lee, P. C., and Kedar-Voivodas, G. "Sex Role and Pupil Role in Early Childhood Education." In L. Katz (ed.), *Current Topics in Early Childhood Education.* Vol. 1. Norwood, N.J.: Ablex, 1977.

Leinbach, M. D., and Fagot, B. I. "Acquisition of Gender Labeling: A Test for Toddlers." *Sex Roles,* 1986, *15,* 655–666.

Levy, G., and Fivush, R. "Scripts and Gender: A New Approach for Examining Gender-Role Development." *Developmental Review,* 1993, *13,* 126–146.

Maccoby, E. E. "Gender as a Social Category." *Developmental Psychology,* 1988, *24,* 755–765.

Maccoby, E. E., and Jacklin, C. N. *The Psychology of Sex Differences.* Stanford, Calif.: Stanford University Press, 1974.

Martin, C. L. "New Directions for Investigating Children's Gender Knowledge." *Developmental Review,* 1993, *13,* 184–204.

O'Brien, M., and Huston, A. C. "Development of Sex-Typed Play Behavior in Toddlers." *Developmental Psychology,* 1985, *21,* 866–871.

Rogoff, B. *Apprenticeship in Thinking: Cognitive Development in a Social Context.* New York: Oxford, 1990.

Serbin, L. A., Connor, J. M., and Citron, C. C. "Sex-Differentiated Free Play Behavior: Effect of Teacher Modeling, Location and Gender." *Developmental Psychology,* 1981, *17,* 640–646.

Serbin, L. A., Connor, J. M., and Iler, I. "Sex-Stereotyped and Nonstereotyped Introductions of New Toys in the Preschool Classroom: An Observational Study of Teacher Behavior and Its Effects." *Psychology of Women Quarterly,* 1979, *4,* 261–265.

Serbin, L. A., O'Leary, K. D., Kent, R. N., and Tonick, I. J. "A Comparison of Teacher Response to Preacademic and Problem Behavior of Boys and Girls. *Child Development,* 1973, *44,* 796–804.

Serbin, L. A., Tonick, I. J., and Sternglanz, S. H. "Shaping Cooperative Cross-Sex Play." *Child Development,* 1977, *48,* 924–929.

Sexton, P. C. "Schools and Effeminacy." *School and Society,* 1968, *96,* 273–274.

Slaby, R. G., and Frey, K. S. "Development of Gender Constancy and Selective Attention to Same-Sex Models." *Child Development,* 1975, *46,* 840–856.

Smith, P. K., and Connolly, K. J. *The Ecology of Preschool Behaviour.* Cambridge, England: Cambridge University Press, 1980.

Trautner, H. M., Helbing, N., and Sahm, W. B. *Schlüssbericht über des VW-Projekt 'Geschlechtstypisierung.'* Frankfurt: Munster, 1985.

Turner, P. J. "Relations Between Attachment, Gender, and Behavior with Peers in Preschool." *Child Development,* 1991, *62,* 1475–1488.

Turner, P. J. "Attachment to Mother and Behaviour with Adults in Preschool." *British Journal of Developmental Psychology,* 1993, *11,* 75–89.

Vroegh, K. "Sex of Teacher and Academic Achievement: A Review of Research." *The Elementary School,* 1976, *76,* 389–405.

Walker, H. M., and McConnell, S. R. *The Walker-McConnell Scale of Social Competence and School Adjustment.* Austin, Tex.: Pro-Ed, 1988.

Whiting, B. B., and Edwards, C. P. *Children of Different Worlds: The Formation of Social Behavior.* Cambridge, Mass.: Harvard University Press, 1988.

Zucker, K. J. "Cross-Gender Identified Children." In B. W. Steinger (ed.), *Gender Dysphoria: Development, Research, Management.* New York: Plenum, 1985.

Zucker, K. J., and Green, R. "Psychosexual Disorders in Children and Adolescents." *Journal of Child Psychology and Psychiatry,* 1992, *33,* 107–151.

BEVERLY I. FAGOT is professor of psychology at the University of Oregon and a research scientist at the Oregon Social Learning Center.

Childhood gender segregation may have consequences for the formation of gendered social norms and close relationships in childhood, adolescence, and adulthood, but parents and teachers may be able to encourage cross-gender contacts and the transcendence of traditional gendered social norms.

Exploring the Consequences of Gender Segregation on Social Relationships

Campbell Leaper

Gender segregation is widely believed by researchers to have important influences on children's development. Because each gender group generally establishes and maintains different norms for social interaction and communication, girls and boys have been described as developing in different "gender cultures" (Carter, 1987; Maccoby, 1990; Maccoby and Jacklin, 1987; Maltz and Borker, 1982; Tannen, 1990; Thorne and Luria, 1986). Earlier chapters in this volume have either reviewed possible explanations for the development of gender segregation (Chapters One, Two, and Three) or described some of the differences in girls' and boys' social interactions that correlate with gender-segregated peer relations (Chapter Four). To complement these efforts, the present chapter considers the possible correlates and consequences of gender segregation beyond early childhood. Parallels will be noted between the gendered social norms that emerge during childhood and those seen in adolescence and adulthood, to illustrate the ways childhood gendered peer relations may establish a script for later adolescent and adult relationship styles (Maccoby, 1990; Thorne and Luria, 1986). Moreover, the way gender differences in social norms may contribute to later communication difficulties and power asymmetries in male-female relationships will be described. Finally, some recommendations for

This work was supported by grants from the Academic Senate (No. 503035–19900) and the Social Sciences Division (No. 443060–09523) of the University of California, Santa Cruz. I would like to thank Margarita Azmitia, Maureen Callanan, Richard Fabes, Beverly Fagot, Eleanor Maccoby, and Carol Martin for comments on earlier drafts of this manuscript. Please direct correspondence to: Campbell Leaper, Department of Psychology, University of California, Santa Cruz, CA 95064. E-mail: cam@cats.ucsc.edu.

parents and teachers interested in encouraging greater equality in gendered social norms will be offered. Also, as I did in the Editor's Notes, I would remind the reader that, although my focus here is on differences between genders, there is also a great deal of variation in sex-typed patterns within each gender (Jacklin, 1981).

Emergence of Gendered Social Norms

To the extent that girls and boys emphasize different patterns of social interaction and activities in their respective peer groups, different norms for social behavior may be expected to emerge (Carter, 1987; Lever, 1976; Maccoby, 1990; Maltz and Borker, 1982; Tannen, 1990; Thorne and Luria, 1986). As Maccoby (1990) has stated, "segregated play groups constitute powerful socialization environments in which children acquire distinctive interaction skills that are adapted to same-sex partners. Sex-typed modes of interaction become consolidated, and . . . the distinctive patterns developed by the two sexes at this time have implications for the same-sex and cross-sex relationships that individuals form as they enter adolescence and adulthood" (p. 516). I shall argue that the patterns of behavior traditionally associated with girls' and boys' same-sex peer groups reflect differences in the expression of affiliation (interpersonal closeness, expressiveness) and assertion (independence, instrumentality). Boys tend to stress self-assertion above affiliation, whereas girls are more likely to demonstrate a stronger motivation for interpersonal closeness, which is coordinated with their simultaneous need for self-assertion (Eckert, 1990; Hughes, 1988; Leaper, 1986, 1991; Sheldon, 1992). One arena in which gender differences in the balance of assertion and affiliation are seen is in children's sex-typed play.

Contexts for Fostering Social Skills and Social Norms. Preferences for sex-typed activities are not strongly related to the initial appearance of same-sex peer preferences (Maccoby and Jacklin, 1987). However, as children get older and their preferences for same-sex peers increase, their play activities often become more sex-typed (see Chapter Four). Researchers taking a contextual-ecological approach to the study of gender have underscored the potential role of sex-typed play activities in promoting different social behaviors and concerns (Etaugh, 1983; Huston, 1985; Lever, 1976; Liss, 1983). Boys' and girls' sex-typed play fosters and reinforces styles of interaction stereotypically associated with either the traditional masculine and or feminine roles (Chapter Four). This appears in more emphasis on self-assertion in boys' play and more stress on affiliation in girls' play.

First, male-stereotyped toys are more likely to foster *independence* and a *task orientation.* For example, traditional boys' toys, such as construction sets, tend to foster self-reliance, object mastery, and problem solving (Block, 1983; Hughes, 1991). In contrast, female-stereotyped toys tend to encourage *interpersonal closeness* and a *social orientation.* For example, traditional girls' toys, such as dolls and kitchen sets, are typically used with one or two other children, inside the home, and near adults (Etaugh, 1983; Hughes, 1991). There is also more talking during girls' play (Chapter Four).

Second, girls' sex-typed play activities help to foster *nurturance* and *affection*. This is most regularly seen in the pretend care of baby dolls. In contrast, boys are more likely than girls to engage in *physically aggressive* forms of play. This includes pretend fights during rough-and-tumble play, aggressive fantasies involving pursuit and conquest during dramatic play, and contact sports such as football (Hughes, 1991; Humphreys and Smith, 1987).

Finally, boys' play activities also place more emphasis on *overt competition* and *dominance* than do girls' activities. Boys' concerns with competition and dominance are especially encouraged during participation in organized sports (Goodwin, 1990; Hughes, 1991; Lever, 1976; Moller, Hymel, and Rubin, 1992; Thorne and Luria, 1986). In contrast, traditionally feminine forms of play foster the development of *social sensitivity*. For example, the characters and scripts in girls' dramatic play are more likely to encourage role taking about realistic settings (for example, playing house) compared to the more fantastic scenarios seen in many boys' pretend play (for example, playing superheroes) (Hughes, 1991). Additionally, play with dress-up toys and clothes underscores many girls' developing sensitivity to physical appearances (Thorne and Luria, 1986).

In summary, the world of play traditionally associated with girls and boys tends to encourage different styles of relating. Girls' sex-typed play reinforces interpersonal closeness, nurturance, talking, and social sensitivity; whereas boys' sex-typed play places more emphasis on independence, task orientation, shared action, and dominance. These different styles of relating, in turn, can be viewed as fostering and maintaining a set of social norms concordant with traditional adult gender roles (Douvan and Adelson, 1966; Lever, 1976). The patterns of social interaction that more broadly define these roles are examined next.

Competition and Dominance. Several researchers have reported that males are more likely than females to establish stable dominance hierarchies within their same-sex peer groups (Goodwin, 1990; Lever, 1976; Pettit, Dodge, Bakshi, and Coie, 1990; Savin-Williams, 1979; Sheldon, 1990; Thorne and Luria, 1986). The greater concern of many males with competition and dominance is reflected in their activities and social interaction styles. First, boys' traditional involvement in team sports provides a basis for establishing rank according to ability (Goodwin, 1990; Hughes, 1991; Thorne and Luria, 1986). Second, boys tend to use more domineering influence strategies such as demands, threats, and physical force than do girls. Girls are more likely to use less direct forms of assertion such as polite requests (Chapter One; Leaper, 1986, 1991; Maccoby and Jacklin, 1987; Miller, Danaher, and Forbes, 1986; Pitcher and Schultz, 1983; Sheldon, 1990). Third, boys engage in competitive conflicts in same-sex interactions more often than do girls (Cairns, Cairns, Neckerman, and Ferguson, 1989; Miller, Danaher, and Forbes, 1986), and this competitiveness may be even greater with friends than nonfriends (Berndt,

1981). Males have been found to compete during even relatively friendly conversations, confronting one another with challenges, mockery, and bravado (Goodwin, 1990; Maltz and Borker, 1982; McCloskey and Coleman, 1992; Pitcher and Schultz, 1983). The general pattern of competition and dominance in many boys' peer groups reflects what Cairns, Cairns, Neckerman, and Ferguson (1989) have called a "brutality norm" (p. 320). Similar findings have been reported for male peer interactions during adulthood (see Maltz and Borker, 1982).

Interpersonal Closeness and Maintaining Harmony. Whereas boys are generally more motivated to attain power and dominance, girls have been found to be more motivated to seek affiliation and closeness (McAdams and Losoff, 1984; Miller, Danaher, and Forbes, 1986). To the extent that forming close ties is valued, maintaining harmony and avoiding discordance become desirable. Girls' concerns with these goals are associated with the development of certain social behaviors. First, there tends to be more emphasis in girls' than boys' groups on being able to read social situations with sensitivity and consideration (Maltz and Borker, 1982; Sheldon, 1990). Second, girls have been found to be more likely than boys to use polite and indirect forms of influence that help to mitigate conflict, such as requests and compromise (Crick and Ladd, 1990; Hartup, French, Laursen, Johnston, and Ogawa, 1993; Miller, Danaher, and Forbes, 1986; Pitcher and Schultz, 1983; Sheldon, 1990, 1992; Weiss and Sachs, 1991; Chapter One). Finally, girls tend to offer more open expressions of support than do boys (Maltz and Borker, 1982; Miller, Danaher, and Forbes, 1986).

The above patterns do not necessarily imply that girls' strivings for affiliation involve the suppression of their self-interest. Instead, it appears that girls are more likely than boys to assert their personal agendas while simultaneously maintaining their connection with others (Eckert, 1990; Leaper, 1986, 1991; Sheldon, 1992). I have referred to this as a "collaborative" social interaction strategy (Leaper, 1986, 1991). It includes, for example, making a proposal for a shared activity. In other cases, girls' coordination of self-assertion and affiliation may not occur simultaneously but within the context of a longer interaction. For example, the coordination may include acting "nice" toward a friend during a competitive game (Hughes, 1988) or combining a set of self-promoting statements about one's accomplishments with a set of other-affirming compliments (Eckert, 1990). This way of addressing the actor's needs for both affiliation and assertion has also been described as "competing in a cooperative mode" (Hughes, 1988, p. 19) or "cooperative competition" (Eckert, 1990, p. 91).

Beyond Simple Dichotomies. While the research finds relatively more emphasis on competition and dominance among boys and on cooperation and harmony among girls, the differences generally are not absolute. Both types of peer groups demonstrate assertion as well as affiliation—although their degree and manner of expression may vary.

For example, some researchers have observed that interpersonal closeness can become a competitive resource in girls' peer relations (Berndt, 1992;

Cairns, Cairns, Neckerman, and Ferguson, 1989; Eckert, 1990; Goodwin, 1990; Lever, 1976; Maltz and Borker, 1982; Thorne and Luria, 1986). Shifts in girls' friendship coalitions have been observed as peer-group members seek to gain acceptance from some while excluding others (Azmitia and Linnet, 1993; Cairns, Cairns, Neckerman, and Ferguson, 1989; Goodwin, 1990; Rauste-von Wright, 1989; Thorne and Luria, 1986). The negotiation of these realignments can involve painful forms of social rejection. For example, in a longitudinal study, Cairns, Cairns, Neckerman, and Ferguson (1989) reported that, by seventh grade, over one-third of female-female conflicts involved manipulation of group acceptance through alienation, ostracism, and character defamation. Corresponding themes of "social aggression" were rarely seen among boys. Thus, somewhat analogously to rank in the traditional male dominance hierarchy, exclusivity becomes a criterion for status in female peer relations.

Just as it would be simplistic to assume that girls are only concerned with affiliation and cooperation, it would be a mistake to characterize boys as favoring only self-assertion and dominance. Forms of affiliation can be seen in boys' traditional same-gender interactions and social relationships. First, the dominance hierarchy itself creates a stable and efficient social organization for group cooperation (Savin-Williams, 1979). Indeed, one of the functions of dominance hierarchies may be to regulate aggression (Strayer and Strayer, 1976) and thereby facilitate group harmony. For example, participation in team sports requires the coordination of interdependent roles directed toward a shared goal. Second, in addition to competitive games, boys' activities are often oriented around tasks that require solutions, such as building a tree house or working on a car. Thus, competitive activities and goal-oriented tasks also become contexts where many boys (and later, men) are able to cooperate with one another. In these various ways, it could be said that many males tend to cooperate in a competitive (or instrumental) mode. Indeed, this is the basis of the masculine ethos of team work. As I will show shortly, the traditional male pattern of seeking affiliation through shared instrumental pursuits has implications for the subsequent development of intimacy in males' close relationships.

Cross-Sex Peer Relations

The emergence of different social norms for affiliation and assertion in same-sex peer groups may contribute to difficulties in later cross-sex relations. Cross-sex interactions may become problematic in older children due to behavioral differences (Chapters One and Four), cognitive factors (Chapters Three and Four), and even emotional style (Chapter Two). For example, gender differences in social influence strategies may make it difficult for girls and boys to get along, and this difficulty may be compounded as girls and boys also begin to form their respective in-group gender identities.

Social Influence Strategies and Beginnings of Male Dominance. Once boys and girls begin to favor different influence strategies, getting along with each other may become problematic. Cross-gender interactions appear especially difficult for females. As previously mentioned, girls are often ineffective in influencing boys if they use the kinds of indirect and polite strategies that they tend to use with one another (see Maccoby, 1990, for a review). Maccoby argues that this is a key reason that girls begin to avoid playing with boys. However, avoiding boys becomes only a partial solution. As elaborated in the rest of this chapter, asymmetries in cross-gender interactions continue throughout childhood and into adolescence and adulthood and may set the stage for communication difficulties in later heterosexual relationships (Gottman, 1993; Tannen, 1990). They may also form the basis for the perpetuation of male dominance (Henley and Kramarae, 1991). The male peer group's emphasis on direct influence strategies may be teaching boys how to be domineering leaders, while the female peer group's emphasis on conflict-mitigation strategies may be teaching girls how to be supportive followers.

In-Group Identity and Gender Boundary Maintenance. With the acquisition of gender categorization, an in-group identity is formed that guides children's behavior (Chapter Three). Although investigators disagree somewhat regarding the extent to which gender categorization and in-group identity account for the initial formation of same-sex peer preferences (compare Chapters One and Three), cognitive factors become increasingly important in the subsequent maintenance and elaboration of gendered peer relations and sex-typed preferences. According to both gender schema theory (Chapter Three) and social identity theory (Archer, 1992), the formation of a concept of gender increases the distinctiveness and positive evaluation of one's own gender group. This leads to a set of corresponding social behaviors aimed at demarcating different groups. Researchers have identified forms of cross-gender interaction, known as either *borderwork* (Thorne and Luria, 1986) or *gender boundary maintenance* (Sroufe and others, 1993), that reaffirm the boundaries and asymmetries between girls' and boys' groups. Those children who regularly violate gender boundary rules tend to be less popular with their peers (Sroufe and others, 1993).

Additionally, boys and girls use various *sexual scripts* to demarcate their respective groups (Maccoby and Jacklin, 1987; Thorne and Luria, 1986), including heterosexual teasing and rituals (Thorne and Luria, 1986). In heterosexual teasing, a boy is charged with liking a girl (or the reverse). In heterosexual rituals, such as cross-sex chasing, girls and boys become separate teams. These chasing games (for example, "cooties") may involve "rituals of pollution" in which the other group (usually of girls) is seen as contaminated. The apparent message underlying sexual scripts is that cross-sex contacts are supposed to occur within the context of heterosexual relationships. Continued adherence to this idea can be seen even after the beginning of heterosexual dating. For most women and men in our culture, cross-sex close relationships are still confined to the sexual-romantic sphere. In this regard, O'Meara (1989) has noted that maintaining cross-sex platonic friendships in adulthood involves confronting ambiguities and challenges from a society where no clear norms exist for this type of relationship. One common challenge is defending a cross-gender friendship to those who tease an individual about sexual motives. Thus, it is often difficult to transcend traditional gender boundaries even in adulthood.

Asymmetries in Borderwork and Gender as Status. Researchers generally find asymmetries between boys and girls in borderwork. First, boys are more likely to initiate and maintain role and group boundaries (Chapter Four; Sroufe and others, 1993; Thorne, 1986; Thorne and Luria, 1986). For example, Fagot (Chapter Four) has found that boys are more likely than girls to receive negative sanctions for cross–sex-typed behavior. These findings are consistent with the corollary of social identity theory that states that high-status groups are more invested than low-status groups in maintaining an in-group identity (Archer, 1992). Second, the characteristics associated with a high-status group are typically valued more than those of a low-status group. Along these lines, studies have found that people generally value traits traditionally associated with being male (independence, assertiveness) more than those traditionally associated with being female (nurturance, compassion) (Broverman and others, 1970). It therefore follows that cross–sex-typed behavior tends to be more common among girls (see Huston, 1983), due to the greater status afforded male-stereotyped characteristics in society. As Feinman (1981) observed, "males experience status loss and females experience status gain in cross-sex-role behavior" (p. 290). Finally, maintaining in-group identity can lead to distorting and devaluing out-group members' behavior. In this regard, the greater status assigned to males has been found to bias children's perceptions of classmates' performance. For example, Lockheed, Harris, and Nemceff (1983) found that school-age children viewed boys as more competent and leader-like than girls, even when objective measures indicated no gender differences in related behaviors. Thus, it appears that children's efforts at borderwork may function to maintain status and social power differences between the sexes in society. Indeed, childhood gender segregation is most rigid in societies with the most gender inequality (Archer, 1992; Whiting and Edwards, 1988).

There are also various institutions that function to perpetuate boundaries between males and females. Among college students, fraternities and sororities generally encourage traditional attitudes about male dominance and female submission. This appears related to the higher incidence of sexual assault among fraternity than nonfraternity men (Kalof and Cargill, 1991; Martin and Hummer, 1989). In later adulthood, "glass ceilings" in the business world as well as gender-segregated organizations and private clubs exist as continuing forms of borderwork that separate females and males.

Physical Appearance and Heterosexual Attractiveness. As they reach adolescence, many girls demonstrate increasing concerns about their physical appearance and heterosexual attractiveness; these concerns reflect some of the lessons of borderwork during childhood. As noted earlier, one lesson is that cross-gender interactions are defined in terms of heterosexual relationships.

Another is that males have a higher status than females. As social identity theory would predict, affiliation with a high-status group becomes desirable to low-status individuals. Correspondingly, girls generally attach greater importance to physical appearance and heterosexual attractiveness than do boys, and these characteristics may become important bases for girls' popularity and competition with other girls during adolescence (Archer, 1992; Douvan and Adelson, 1966; Eder and Sanford, 1986; Feinman, 1981; Hill and Lynch, 1983; Rauste-von Wright, 1989; Thorne and Luria, 1986). Although girls' popularity with boys often affects their status with other girls, boys' popularity with girls is less likely to relate to their status with other boys (Archer, 1992; Douvan and Adelson, 1966; Hill and Lynch, 1983; Rauste-von Wright, 1989; Thorne and Luria, 1986).

Asymmetries in girls' and boys' concerns with heterosexual attractiveness appear to have other impacts as well. Beginning in adolescence, many girls view popularity with boys as incompatible with doing well in academic, athletic, and other instrumental pursuits (see Hill and Lynch, 1983). Perhaps as a consequence, adolescent girls' performance in these areas shows a sharp decline. For example, Feiring and Lewis (1991) reported that adolescent girls' academic competence was negatively related to their amount of contact with cross-sex friends. In contrast, there was no correlation between boys' academic competence and their amount of contact with cross-sex friends. Feiring and Lewis suggested that girls may tend to inhibit their displays of academic competence as well as their interest in academic achievement when with boys. They also found that boys' social competence was positively correlated with their amount of contact with cross-sex friends. The same correlation for girls was not significant. Thus, it would appear that the boys derived more positive gains from cross-sex relationships than did the girls. As happens in many traditional heterosexual relations, examined in the next section, perhaps the males in this study benefited from the support of their female companions but did not reciprocate.

Development and Expression of Intimacy. Gendered social norms in childhood can be viewed as paving the way for later gender differences in intimacy during adolescence and adulthood (Maccoby, 1990; Thorne and Luria, 1986). Thorne and Luria have commented that "coming to adolescent sexual intimacy from different and asymmetric gender subcultures, girls and boys bring somewhat different needs, capacities, and types of knowledge" (p. 188). As previously described, girls' childhood peer groups place more emphasis on social sensitivity and responsiveness in dyads or small groups, while the peer world of boys is based more on activity and competition in large groups. These patterns parallel those reported for females and males during adolescence and adulthood. Adolescent girls tend to attach more importance to intimacy and equality in friendships than do adolescent boys (Berndt, 1992; Eder and Sanford, 1986; Maltz and Borker, 1982; McAdams and Losoff, 1984; Youniss and Smollar, 1985). Also, friendship processes related to intimacy—such as mutual self-disclosure, supportiveness, and perspective taking—tend to emerge earlier and be seen more regularly in the friendships of adolescent girls (Berndt, 1992; Buhrmester and Furman, 1987; Burleson, 1982; Camarena, Sarigiani, and Petersen, 1990; Eder and Sanford, 1986; Jones and Denbo, 1989; Selman and others, 1986; Sharabany, Gershoni, and Hofman, 1981; Thorne and Luria, 1986; Youniss and Smollar, 1985). Females' greater concern with intimacy and self-disclosure in friendship appears to continue into adulthood (Aries, 1987; Dindia and Allen, 1992; Mazur, 1989) and into old age (Powers and Bultena, 1976).

Boys' traditional childhood peer relations may not prepare them as well for the demands of intimate friendship in adolescence and adulthood. One possibility is that the typically larger size of boys' peer groups provides more anonymity than the one-on-one relationships common among girls (Berndt, 1992; Thorne and Luria, 1986) and gives boys less experience in expressing and talking about difficult emotions by the time they reach adolescence (see Block, 1983). A related possibility is that traditional males and females both establish intimacy in their friendships but in different ways. Whereas *self-disclosure* appears to be the primary pathway toward intimacy in adolescent girls' friendships, *shared activity* may be an alternative pathway to intimacy for adolescent boys. (Buhrmester and Furman, 1987; Camarena, Sarigiani, and Petersen, 1990; Eder and Sanford, 1986; Hill and Lynch, 1983; Lever, 1976; Sharabany, Gershoni, and Hofman, 1981; Thorne and Luria, 1986; Youniss and Smollar, 1985). Friendship intimacy based on shared activity is similar to many boys' use of sports as a focus for their peer relations. In both cases, the relationship is defined in terms of "doing things" together. These shared activities may provide "rules and roles [that] structure a threatening situation of potential intimacy into a safe and less personal one in which males can express their affiliative needs" (Mazur, 1989, p. 279). (However, it may be that friendships based in self-disclosure still reflect a deeper level of intimacy and shared understanding than those based on shared activities alone.)

These interpretations suggest that traditional males may have less *competence* or *ability* than females in expressiveness. An alternative explanation, however, is that observed gender differences in intimacy-related behaviors are due to differences in *preference* (Reis, Senchak, and Solomon, 1985; Winstead, 1986). One factor that writers have especially noted in this regard is that males continue to be more concerned with power and dominance than their female counterparts during adolescence (Eder and Sanford, 1986; Maltz and Borker, 1982; McAdams and Losoff, 1984; Savin-Williams, 1979). Consequently, many adolescent and adult males may be reluctant to express personal feelings and information with one another because they perceive it as a potential sign of vulnerability and an opportunity for the other to take the advantage (Aries, 1987; Lewis, 1978; Sattel, 1983). They may also have fears of appearing homosexual (Lewis, 1978). Thus, male inexpressiveness may sometimes function to maintain independence and dominance. As Sattel (1983) commented, "men talk, but they always need a reason—and that reason often amounts to another effort at establishing who *really* is best, stronger, smarter, or ultimately, more powerful" (p. 122).

Support for the idea that male inexpressiveness may be due more to preference than ability comes from studies finding that many adolescent and adult males are more likely to disclose with female than male partners (Reisman, 1990; Winstead, 1986; Youniss and Smollar, 1985). The nurturance and submission traditionally associated with the female role may reduce males' self-presentation concerns regarding power and dominance. Also, males may feel more secure about their status and power with female than with male peers. Along these lines, Barth and Kinder (1988) observed that men are more likely than women to form different relationships to meet different needs. Thus, adolescent and adult males may turn toward their female friends to meet their intimacy needs, while using their male friends for their various instrumental needs. If males are not encouraging females' instrumental pursuits, then the benefits of cross-gender relationships may be asymmetrical for women and men.

A Study of Self-Disclosure and Support

The gender differences in the role of self-disclosure in the formation of emotional closeness and in the responsiveness and support males and females give to one another were considered in a recent study that Mary Carson, Carrie Baker, Heithre Holliday, and I carried out to examine self-disclosure processes and intimacy in the conversations of same- and cross-sex young adult friends (Leaper, Carson, Baker, and Holliday, under review). The postadolescent years are an important period in the development of intimacy in both same- and cross-sex friendships (Fischer, 1981). Accordingly, we examined conversational processes in both types of friendships.

Sample and Procedure. The research was carried out with pairs of college undergraduates eighteen to twenty-one years old (mean age = nineteen years) attending a California university in a politically liberal community. There were twenty female-female pairs, twenty female-male pairs, and nineteen male-male pairs. Members of each pair had known one another for at least two months (mean length of friendship = twelve months).

Each pair was seated together in a university research office for four conversation sessions. For each session, the two friends were left in the room by themselves while their conversation was audiotaped. First, they were asked to talk about whatever they wanted. Thereafter, they were assigned three specific topics in counterbalanced order across friendship pairs. The present discussion centers on their discussion of a single topic: how their family relations had changed since they entered college. Transcripts of the recordings were coded for the incidence of personal self-disclosures and various listening responses. We used Morton's (1978) definition of self-disclosure as private facts or personal feelings, and we adapted Burleson's (1982) comforting communication strategies to classify listeners' responses to partners' self-disclosures. Responses ranged from being highly unresponsive and unsupportive to being highly responsive and supportive and were coded as follows: *resistance* (for example, criticizing), *abstain* (nonresponsive), *back channel listening response* ("mm hm"), *simple acknowledgment* ("that sounds hard"), *clarification question* ("When did that occur?"), *explaining* (for example, rationalizing), and *active understanding* (for example, reflecting on the partner's experience). Intercoder reliabilities for these coding categories were high (average kappa coefficient = .82; minimum kappa = .65).

Findings and Interpretations. There were no group differences in the incidence of self-disclosure. This finding is consistent with other reports indicating that gender differences in amounts of self-disclosure are reduced when the context is controlled (Shaffer, Pegalis, and Cornell, 1992). It also lends support to the interpretation that past reports of gender differences in self-disclosure are due more to the participants' behavioral preferences than their actual abilities (see Reis, Senchak, and Solomon, 1985; Winstead, 1986). When placed in a context that demands self-disclosure, men appear to indicate that they can express personal thoughts and feelings, even though many of them may choose not to do this with one another.

Being able to offer personal information about one's self when requested may be a relatively simple conversational skill. In contrast, our findings suggested that providing responsive and supportive feedback may demand more complex social skills less affected by situational variables. Giving appropriate feedback may require more sophistication in terms of knowing what to say and when to say it. We found gender-related differences in the use of response types at the two extremes of responsiveness. In particular, there were significant group differences in the use of abstains and active understanding. There were no differences associated with resistance, back channels, simple acknowledgments, clarification questions, or explaining.

Active understanding was significantly more likely in the female pairs (M = 23 percent) than in either the male pairs (M = 13 percent) or mixed pairs (M = 11 percent) (p < .02 and .004, respectively). This finding is consistent with studies indicating a greater use of supportive communication by women than men (Aries, 1987; Tannen, 1990; West and Zimmerman, 1985).

Abstaining responses to partner self-disclosures were more likely in the male pairs (M = 27 percent) than in either the female pairs (M = 16 percent) or the mixed pairs (M = 17 percent) (both p < .02). This finding is consistent with other reports indicating that men tend to be less responsive and supportive during conversation than women (see Aries, 1987; Tannen, 1990; West and Zimmerman, 1985).

In order to identify any differences between males and females within the mixed pairs in the use of abstaining and active understanding responses, separate analyses were carried out with these dyads, using partner as a within-group factor. These analyses revealed that there were no significant differences between female and male partners in the mixed pairs in their proportions of abstaining responses (M = 16 percent and M = 18 percent, respectively) or active understanding (M = 9 percent and M = 12 percent, respectively). Thus, men's use of abstaining responses and women's use of active understanding were proportionally higher in the same-sex than the mixed-sex friendship pairs.

The absence of gender differences regarding abstaining responses within the cross-sex friendship pairs runs counter to some studies that have reported a greater incidence of male than female unresponsiveness in heterosexual relationships (Cunningham, Braiker, and Kelley, 1982; McLaughlin, Cody, Kane, and Robey, 1981; West and Zimmerman, 1985). Perhaps this discrepancy is due to our use of friends as opposed to romantic partners. There have been few observational studies of cross-gender platonic friends, but since this type of relationship involves breaking traditional gender boundaries, persons who maintain these friendships may tend to be less sex-typed in their social behavior than others.

Our findings regarding the overall incidence of self-disclosure indicate that, when asked to talk about a personal topic, females and males can disclose equal amounts. The observed gender-related differences in responses to this self-disclosure were more ambiguous. That the males in both the same- and mixed-sex pairs used fewer active understanding responses than the females in same-sex pairs suggests either that the males were less skilled in this kind of response or that they had a very strong preference against using it in both settings. Research on children and adolescents has indicated that males are less likely than females to demonstrate competence in supportive and responsive communication skills (Black and Hazen, 1990; Burleson, 1982; Leaper, 1991). However, it is still possible that males may simply choose not to respond extensively to their friends' disclosures, based on a belief that it is somehow inappropriate for them to do so (for example, because it would embarrass the friend) (Perlman and Fehr, 1987).

Another finding that allows for different interpretations regarding ability versus preference is that females used fewer active understanding responses and males used fewer abstaining responses in the mixed-sex dyads than in the same-sex dyads. One possible interpretation is that the partner's gender made a difference. Perhaps males are less apt to use abstains and females are more apt to use active understanding responses with female than male friends. This would be consistent with the proposal that males and females alike are more disclosing and intimate with female friends (see Winstead, 1986). Alternatively, there may be inherent differences among our sample of friends. Perhaps persons who participated in the study with cross-sex friends were different in either their social skills (or preferences) than those who participated with same-sex friends. These kinds of questions can be addressed in future research. As O'Meara (1989) has emphasized, we currently know relatively little about cross-gender friendships.

Our research highlights some of the ways that gendered social patterns in childhood may affect the quality of intimate relationships in adulthood. For example, the tendency for females to be more overtly responsive and supportive than males during intimate discussions has implications for our understanding of how women and men relate (or fail to relate) in later marital relationships. An accumulating number of studies indicate that imbalances in self-disclosure and emotional support are related to marital dissatisfaction (Hendrick, 1981), marital distress and divorce (Christensen and Heavey, 1990; Gottman, 1993), and domestic violence (Babcock, Waltz, Jacobson, and Gottman, 1993). It would therefore appear that traditional sex-role pathways linked to gender segregation may limit and sometimes even impair the quality of later social-emotional adjustment (Bem, 1983; Block, 1973; Kaplan and Sedney, 1980). The logical implication of this conclusion is to seek ways to transcend gender segregation and encourage gender equality.

Transcending Gender Segregation

In this chapter, I have argued that gender segregation fosters, extends, and consolidates sex-typed play activities and social norms. As a consequence, girls and boys learn to adopt different concerns and competencies, a circumstance that may limit individuals' full potential and may also lead to imbalances in status and power for females and males. Cross-cultural research indicates a positive correlation between childhood gender segregation and the degree of gender inequality in the society (see Archer, 1992; Whiting and Edwards, 1988). It would therefore appear that gender segregation and gendered social norms function to reinforce one another.

When girls and boys have been encouraged to play with one another, a reduction in sex-typing has been observed (Bianchi and Bakeman, 1983; Cherry-Wilkinson, Lindow, and Chiang, 1985; Serbin, Tonick, and Sternglanz, 1977). However, contact alone is not sufficient to reduce sex-typing and gender segregation (Maccoby and Jacklin, 1987). How cross-gender interactions are organized is also important. The research literature suggests various strategies that interested parents and teachers might apply.

Recommendations for Parents. First, researchers have noted some naturally occurring situations during which the salience of gender and gender roles is reduced and cross-sex peer interactions are more likely. These include adult-structured activities; absorbing tasks requiring cooperation; and private settings, such as children's homes (Thorne, 1986).

Second, children have been found to hold fewer gender stereotypes when their parents model nontraditional roles: for example, when mothers are employed outside the home (Hoffman, 1989) or fathers are actively involved in the children's care and nurturance (Miedzian, 1991).

Third, parents can provide their children with alternative or "subversive" ideas about gender. Bem (1983) proposed that "such alternative schemata 'build up one's resistance' to the lessons of the dominant culture and thereby enable one to remain gender-aschematic even while living in a gender-schematic society" (p. 610). Although there are no data regarding the effectiveness of this strategy, African-American parents have been found to use a similar technique with their children to prepare them for racism (Thornton, Chatters, Taylor, and Allen, 1990).

Fourth, Bem (1989) has also argued that teaching children the relation between genitalia and gender assignment can reduce gender stereotyping. Children with this understanding are able to realize that the distinction between male and female is not based on other physical or psychological characteristics. This allows the child to reason that "it is my body, not my behavior, that makes me either a male or a female; hence I can behave in any way that I please" (Bem, 1989, p. 661). Perhaps the resulting flexibility would include playing with children of the other gender.

Fifth, Fagot (Chapter Four) has noted how stereotypically feminine clothing can limit girls' activities. Girls are more easily able to engage in a wider range of activities if they are dressed in overalls and sneakers (like boys). Moreover, less emphasis will be placed on differences in physical appearance this way.

Sixth, parents and other family members may want to provide extra support for the development of cross-sex-typed competencies. This would mean reinforcing daughters in instrumental areas and sons in relational areas. Children will likely get plenty of encouragement to excel in sex-typed domains from various socialization agents (Huston, 1983). However, parents and extended family may be the only important sources for fostering instrumental competence in girls and expressive competence in boys. Indeed, one longitudinal study of adolescent development found that higher ego levels (believed to be associated with gender-role transcendence) were more likely in daughters whose parents had earlier emphasized independence and in sons whose parents had earlier emphasized closeness (see Leaper and others, 1989).

Finally, limiting children's television viewing may be helpful, since most programming has been found to depict traditional gender stereotypes. Although no causal link has been established, studies indicate a positive correlation between children's amount of television viewing and their degree of gender stereotyping (Calvert and Huston, 1987).

Recommendations for Teachers. Most of the techniques suggested for parents may also be invoked by teachers. However, there are some additional strategies that teachers can implement, given the relatively controlled social environment of the classroom. First, teachers can directly reinforce cross-sex interactions (Bianchi and Bakeman, 1983; Serbin, Tonick, and Sternglanz, 1977). For example, the *jigsaw classroom,* in which teachers arrange cooperative activities that require the interdependence of group members, has been proven successful in increasing intergroup affiliations (Aronson and others, 1978). However, teachers need to encourage cross-sex contacts throughout the year; otherwise, children tend to revert to their previous sex-typed patterns (Serbin, Tonick, and Sternglanz, 1977).

Second, teachers can arrange training programs that counter stereotypical models (Katz and Walsh, 1991; Lockheed, Harris, and Nemceff, 1983). For example, Lockheed, Harris, and Nemceff went into fourth- and fifth-grade classrooms and assigned children to an "expectation training program" in which girls were trained in a complex task and then modeled as leaders to others. This intervention was found to improve peer perceptions of girls' competence relative to boys'.

Third, teachers can avoid using children's gender to organize space and activities. Lloyd and Duveen's (1992) study of children's first year of school indicated that this was a common practice even among teachers who made a conscious effort to avoid sexism. For example, teachers asked children to form separate "boys'" and "girls'" lines at playtime and used the terms "boys" and "girls" separately in the management of children's behavior ("Boys, calm down!").

Finally, teachers can arrange for cooperative play in both female- and male-stereotyped play settings. Research indicates that when given the same toys, girls and boys behave in highly similar ways (Pellegrini and Perlmutter, 1989). Also, the degree to which activity is structured by either adults or peers appears to matter (Chapter Four; Carpenter, 1983). Adult-structured activities tend to stress compliance more and initiative less than peer-directed activities. Boys typically receive less adult structure and engage in more peer structure than girls (Carpenter, 1983). Therefore, a related strategy is to provide girls and boys with both peer- and adult-structured activities in order to encourage greater balance in girls' and boys' social norms and skills.

Conclusion

The foregoing review has focused on socialization patterns that contribute to gender differences in social behavior and has presented new research evidence to illustrate the possible impact of gendered social norms on conversational intimacy and support between same- and cross-sex pairs of young adult friends.

As I have shown, several factors appear to account for variations in the relationships between children's peer relations and degrees of sex-typing, and in order to better appreciate the complexities of gender and its construction in development, researchers need to continue their efforts aimed at identifying factors related to traditional as well as nontraditional gender pathways. Relevant aspects of the interactive context include sociometric status (Azmitia and Linnet, 1993; Crick and Ladd, 1990), age level (Black, 1992; Coie, Dodge, Terry, and Wright, 1991), the activity setting (Huston, 1985; Pellegrini and Perlmutter, 1989), partner gender (Leaper, 1991; Miller, Danaher, and Forbes, 1986; Moely, Skarin, and Weil, 1979), economic background (Eckert, 1988; Eder, 1990), and cultural traditions (Whiting and Edwards, 1988). Additionally, longitudinal studies would be especially useful in tracking the consequences of gender segregation on later social relations as well as in identifying possible trajectories leading to gender-role transcendence (for examples, see Feiring and Lewis, 1991; Leaper and others, 1989).

References

Archer, J. "Childhood Gender Roles: Social Context and Organisation." In H. McGurk (ed.), *Childhood Social Development: Contemporary Perspectives.* Hove, England: Erlbaum, 1992.

Aries, E. J. "Gender and Communication." In P. Shaver and C. Hendrick (eds.), *Review of Personality and Social Psychology.* Vol. 7. Newbury Park: Calif.: Sage, 1987.

Aronson, E., Stephan, C., Sikes, J., Blaney, N., and Snapp, M. *The Jigsaw Classroom.* Newbury Park, Calif.: Sage, 1978.

Azmitia, M., and Linnet, J. "Elementary School Children's Conflicts with Friends and Acquaintances." Unpublished paper, Department of Psychology, University of California, Santa Cruz, 1993.

Babcock, J. C., Waltz, J., Jacobson, N. S., and Gottman, J. M. "Power and Violence: The Relation Between Communication Patterns, Power Discrepancies, and Domestic Violence." *Journal of Consulting and Clinical Psychology,* 1993, *61,* 40–50.

Barth, R. J., and Kinder, B. N. "A Theoretical Analysis of Sex Differences in Same-Sex Friendships." *Sex Roles,* 1988, *19,* 349–363.

Bem, S. L. "Gender Schema Theory and Its Implications for Child Development: Raising Gender-Aschematic Children in a Gender-Schematic Society." *Signs: Journal of Women in Culture and Society,* 1983, *8,* 598–616.

Bem, S. L. "Genital Knowledge and Gender Constancy in Preschool Children." *Child Development,* 1989, *60,* 649–662.

Berndt, T. J. "Effects of Friendship on Prosocial Intentions and Behavior." *Child Development,* 1981, *52,* 636–643.

Berndt, T. J. "Friendship and Friends' Influence in Adolescence." *Current Directions in Psychological Science,* 1992, *1,* 156–159.

Bianchi, B. D., and Bakeman, R. "Patterns of Sex Typing in an Open School." In M. B. Liss (ed.), *Social and Cognitive Skills: Sex Roles and Children's Play.* San Diego: Academic Press, 1983.

Black, B. "Negotiating Social Pretend Play: Communication Differences Related to Social Status and Sex." *Merrill-Palmer Quarterly,* 1992, *38,* 212–232.

Black, B., and Hazen, N. L. "Social Status and Patterns of Communication in Acquainted and Unacquainted Preschool Children." *Developmental Psychology,* 1990, *26,* 379–387.

Block, J. H. "Conceptions of Sex Role: Some Cross-Cultural and Longitudinal Perspectives." *American Psychologist,* 1973, *28,* 512–526.

Block, J. H. "Differential Premises Arising from Differential Socialization of the Sexes: Some Conjectures." *Child Development,* 1983, *54,* 1335–1354.

Broverman, I. K., Broverman, D. M., Clarkson, F. E., Rosenkrantz, P. S., and Vogel, S. R. "Sex-Role Stereotypes and Clinical Judgments of Mental Health." *Journal of Consulting and Clinical Psychology,* 1970, *34,* 1–7.

Buhrmester, D., and Furman, W. "The Development of Companionship and Intimacy." *Child Development,* 1987, *58,* 1101–1113.

Burleson, B. R. "The Development of Comforting Communication Skills in Childhood and Adolescence." *Child Development,* 1982, *53,* 1578–1588.

Cairns, R. B., Cairns, B. D., Neckerman, H. J., and Ferguson, L. L. "Growth and Aggression: 1. Childhood to Early Adolescence." *Developmental Psychology,* 1989, *25,* 320–330.

Calvert, S. L., and Huston, A. C. "Television and Children's Gender Schemata." In L. S. Liben and M. L. Signorella (eds.), *Children's Gender Schemata.* New Directions for Child Development, no. 38. San Francisco: Jossey-Bass, 1987.

Camarena, P. M., Sarigiani, P. A., and Petersen, A. C. "Gender-Specific Pathways to Intimacy in Early Adolescence." *Journal of Youth and Adolescence,* 1990, *19,* 19–32.

Carpenter, C. J. "Activity Structure and Play: Implications for Socialization." In M. B. Liss (ed.), *Social and Cognitive Skills: Sex Roles and Children's Play.* San Diego: Academic Press, 1983.

Carter, D. B. "The Roles of Peers in Sex Role Socialization." In D. B. Carter (ed.), *Current Conceptions of Sex Roles and Sex Typing: Theory and Research.* New York: Praeger, 1987.

Cherry-Wilkinson, L., Lindow, J., and Chiang, C.-P. "Sex Differences and Sex Segregation in Students' Small-Group Communication." In L. Cherry-Wilkinson and C. B. Marrett (eds.), *Gender Influences in Classroom Interaction.* San Diego: Academic Press, 1985.

Christensen, A., and Heavey, C. L. "Gender and Social Structure in the Demand/Withdraw Pattern of Marital Interaction." *Journal of Personality and Social Psychology,* 1990, *59,* 73–81.

Coie, J. D., Dodge, K. A., Terry, R., and Wright, V. "The Role of Aggression in Peer Relations: An Analysis of Aggression Episodes in Boys' Play Groups." *Child Development,* 1991, *62,* 812–826.

Crick, N. R., and Ladd, G. W. "Children's Perceptions of the Outcomes of Social Strategies: Do the Ends Justify Being Mean?" *Developmental Psychology,* 1990, *26,* 612–620.

Cunningham, J. D., Braiker, H., and Kelley, H. H. "Marital-Status and Sex Differences in Problems Reported by Married and Cohabiting Couples." *Psychology of Women Quarterly,* 1982, *64,* 415–427.

Dindia, K., and Allen, M. "Sex Differences in Self-Disclosure: A Meta-Analysis." *Psychological Bulletin,* 1992, *112,* 106–124.

Douvan, E., and Adelson, J. *The Adolescent Experience.* New York: Wiley, 1966.

Eckert, P. "Adolescent Social Structure and the Spread of Linguistic Change." *Language in Society,* 1988, *17,* 183–208.

Eckert, P. "Cooperative Competition in Adolescent 'Girl Talk.'" *Discourse Processes,* 1990, *13,* 91–122.

Eder, D. "Serious and Playful Disputes: Variation in Conflict Talk Among Female Adolescents." In A. D. Grimshaw (ed.), *Conflict Talk: Sociolinguistic Investigations of Arguments in Conversations.* Cambridge, England: Cambridge University Press, 1990.

Eder, D., and Sanford, S. "The Development and Maintenance of Interactional Norms Among Early Adolescents." In P. Adler and P. Adler (eds.), *Sociological Studies of Child Development.* Greenwich, Conn.: JAI Press, 1986.

Etaugh, C. "The Influence of Environmental Factors on Sex Differences in Children's Play." In M. B. Liss (ed.), *Social and Cognitive Skills: Sex Roles and Children's Play.* San Diego: Academic Press, 1983.

Feinman, S. "Why Is Cross-Sex-Role Behavior More Approved for Girls Than for Boys? A Status Characteristic Approach." *Sex Roles,* 1981, *7,* 289–300.

Feiring, C., and Lewis, M. "The Transition from Middle Childhood to Early Adolescence: Sex Differences in the Social Network and Perceived Self-Competence." *Sex Roles,* 1991, *24,* 489–509.

Fischer, J. L. "Transitions in Relationship Style from Adolescence to Young Adulthood." *Journal of Youth and Adolescence,* 1981, *10,* 11–23.

Goodwin, M. H. "Tactical Uses of Stories: Participation Frameworks Within Girls' and Boys' Disputes." *Discourse Processes,* 1990, *13,* 33–71.

Gottman, J. M. "The Roles of Conflict Engagement, Escalation, and Avoidance in Marital Interaction: A Longitudinal View of Five Types of Couples." *Journal of Consulting and Clinical Psychology,* 1993, *61,* 6–15.

Hartup, W. W., French, D. C., Laursen, B., Johnston, M. K., and Ogawa, J. R. "Conflict and Friendship Relations in Middle Childhood: Behavior in a Close-Field Situation." *Child Development,* 1993, *64,* 445–454.

Hendrick, S. S. "Self-Disclosure and Marital Satisfaction." *Journal of Personality and Social Psychology,* 1981, *40,* 1150–1159.

Henley, N. M., and Kramarae, C. "Gender, Power, and Miscommunication." In N. Coupland, H. Giles, and J. M. Wiemann (eds.), *"Miscommunication" and Problematic Talk.* Newbury Park, Calif.: Sage, 1991.

Hill, J. P., and Lynch, M. E. "The Intensification of Gender-Related Role Expectations During Early Adolescence." In J. Brooks-Gunn and A. C. Petersen (eds.), *Girls at Puberty: Biological and Psychological Perspectives.* New York: Plenum, 1983.

Hoffman, L. W. "Effects of Maternal Employment in the Two-Parent Family." *American Psychologist,* 1989, *44,* 283–292.

Hughes, F. P. *Children, Play, and Development.* Boston: Allyn & Bacon, 1991.

Hughes, L. A. "'But That's Not Really Mean': Competing in a Cooperative Mode." *Sex Roles,* 1988, *19,* 669–687.

Humphreys, A. P., and Smith, P. K. "Rough and Tumble, Friendship, and Dominance in School Children: Evidence for Continuity and Change with Age." *Child Development,* 1987, *58,* 201–212.

Huston, A. C. "Sex-Typing." In P. H. Mussen (ed.), *Handbook of Child Psychology.* (4th ed.) Vol. 4: *Socialization, Personality, and Social Development.* (E. M. Hetherington, vol. ed.) New York: Wiley, 1983.

Huston, A. C. "The Development of Sex-Typing: Themes from Recent Research." *Developmental Review,* 1985, *5,* 1–17.

Jacklin, C. N. "Methodological Issues in the Study of Sex-Related Differences." *Developmental Review,* 1981, *1,* 266–273.

Jones, G. P., and Denbo, M. H. "Age and Sex Role Differences in Intimate Friendships During Childhood and Adolescence." *Merrill-Palmer Quarterly,* 1989, *35,* 445–462.

Kalof, L., and Cargill, T. "Fraternity and Sorority Membership and Gender Dominance Attitudes." *Sex Roles,* 1991, *25,* 417–423.

Kaplan, A. G., and Sedney, M. A. *Psychology and Sex Roles: An Androgynous Perspective.* Boston: Little, Brown, 1980.

Katz, P. A., and Walsh, P. V. "Modification of Children's Gender-Stereotyped Behavior." *Child Development,* 1991, *62,* 338–351.

Leaper, C. "The Sequential Patterning of Agency and Communion in Children's Talk: Differences Associated with Age, Speaker Gender, and Partner Gender." Unpublished doctoral dissertation, Department of Psychology, University of California at Los Angeles, 1986.

Leaper, C. "Influence and Involvement in Children's Discourse: Age, Gender, and Partner Effects." *Child Development,* 1991, *62,* 797–811.

Leaper, C., Carson, M., Baker, C., and Holliday, H. "Self-Disclosure and Listener Support in Same- and Cross-Gender Friends' Conversations." Under review.

Leaper, C., Hauser, S. T., Kremen, A., Powers, S. I., Jacobson, A. M., Noam, G. G., Weiss-Perry, B., and Follansbee, D. "Adolescent-Parent Interactions in Relation to Adolescents' Gender and Ego Development Pathway: A Longitudinal Study." *Journal of Early Adolescence,* 1989, *9,* 335–361.

Lever, J. "Sex Differences in the Games Children Play." *Social Problems,* 1976, *23,* 478–487.

Lewis, R. A. "Emotional Intimacy Among Men." *Journal of Social Issues,* 1978, *34,* 108–121.

Liss, M. B. "Learning Gender-Related Skills Through Play." In M. B. Liss (ed.), *Social and Cognitive Skills: Sex Roles and Children's Play.* San Diego: Academic Press, 1983.

Lloyd, B., and Duveen, G. *Gender Identities and Education: The Impact of Starting School.* New York: St. Martin's Press, 1992.

Lockheed, M. E., Harris, A. M., and Nemceff, W. P. "Sex and Social Influence: Does Sex Function as a Status Characteristic in Mixed-Sex Groups of Children?" *Journal of Educational Psychology,* 1983, *75,* 877–888.

McAdams, D. P., and Losoff, M. "Friendship Motivation in Fourth and Sixth Graders: A Thematic Analysis." *Journal of Social and Personal Relationships,* 1984, *1,* 11–27.

McCloskey, L. A., and Coleman, L. M. "Difference Without Dominance: Children's Talk in Mixed- and Same-Sex Dyads." *Sex Roles,* 1992, *27,* 241–257.

Maccoby, E. E. "Gender and Relationships: A Developmental Account." *American Psychologist,* 1990, *45,* 513–520.

Maccoby, E. E., and Jacklin, C. N. "Gender Segregation in Childhood." In H. W. Reese (ed.), *Advances in Child Development and Behavior.* Vol. 20. San Diego: Academic Press, 1987.

McLaughlin, M. L., Cody, M. J., Kane, M. L., and Robey, C. S. "Sex Differences in Story Receipt and Story Sequencing Behaviors in Dyadic Conversations." *Human Communication Research,* 1981, *7,* 99–116.

Maltz, D. N., and Borker, R. A. "A Cultural Approach to Male-Female Miscommunication." In J. J. Gumperz (ed.), *Language and Social Identity*. New York: Cambridge University Press, 1982.

Martin, P. Y., and Hummer, R. A. "Fraternities and Rape on Campus." *Gender and Society*, 1989, *3*, 457–473.

Mazur, E. "Predicting Gender Differences in Same-Sex Friendships from Affiliation Motive and Value." *Psychology of Women Quarterly*, 1989, *13*, 277–291.

Miedzian, M. *Boys Will Be Boys: Breaking the Link Between Masculinity and Violence*. New York: Doubleday, 1991.

Miller, P. M., Danaher, D. L., and Forbes, D. "Sex-Related Strategies for Coping with Interpersonal Conflict in Children Aged Five to Seven." *Developmental Psychology*, 1986, *22*, 543–548.

Moely, B. E., Skarin, K., and Weil, S. "Sex Differences in Competition-Cooperation Behavior of Children at Two Age Levels." *Sex Roles*, 1979, *5*, 329–342.

Moller, L. C., Hymel, S., and Rubin, K. H. "Sex Typing in Play and Popularity in Middle Childhood." *Sex Roles*, 1992, *26*, 331–353.

Morton, T. L. "Intimacy and Reciprocity of Exchange: A Comparison of Spouses and Strangers." *Journal of Personality and Social Psychology*, 1978, *36*, 72–81.

O'Meara, J. D. "Cross-Sex Friendship: Four Basic Challenges of an Ignored Relationship." *Sex Roles*, 1989, *21*, 525–543.

Pellegrini, A. D., and Perlmutter, J. C. "Classroom Contextual Effects on Children's Play." *Developmental Psychology*, 1989, *25*, 289–296.

Perlman, D., and Fehr, B. "The Development of Intimate Relationships." In D. Perlman and S. Duck (eds.), *Intimate Relationships: Development, Dynamics, and Deterioration*. Newbury Park, Calif.: Sage, 1987.

Pettit, G. S., Dodge, K. A., Bakshi, A., and Coie, J. D. "The Emergence of Social Dominance in Young Boys' Play Groups: Developmental Differences in Behavioral Correlates." *Developmental Psychology*, 1990, *26*, 1017–1025.

Pitcher, E. G., and Schultz, L. H. *Boys and Girls at Play: The Development of Sex Roles*. New York: Praeger, 1983.

Powers, E. A., and Bultena, G. L. "Sex Differences in Intimate Friendships of Old Age." *Journal of Marriage and the Family*, 1976, *38*, 739–747.

Rauste-von Wright, M. "Physical and Verbal Aggression in Peer Groups Among Finnish Adolescent Boys and Girls." *International Journal of Behavioral Development*, 1989, *12*, 473–484.

Reis, H. T., Senchak, M., and Solomon, B. "Sex Differences in the Intimacy of Social Interaction: Further Examination of Potential Explanations." *Journal of Personality and Social Psychology*, 1985, *48*, 1204–1217.

Reisman, J. M. "Intimacy in Same-Sex Friendships." *Sex Roles*, 1990, *23*, 65–82.

Sattel, J. W. "Men, Inexpressiveness, and Power." In B. Thorne, C. Kramarae, and N. Henley (eds.), *Language, Gender, and Society*. Rowley, Mass.: Newbury House, 1983.

Savin-Williams, R. C. "Dominance Hierarchies in Groups of Early Adolescents." *Child Development*, 1979, *50*, 923–935.

Selman, R. L., Beardslee, W. R., Schultz, L. H., Krupa, M., and Podorefsky, D. "Assessing Adolescent Interpersonal Negotiation Strategies: Toward the Integration of Structural and Functional Models." *Developmental Psychology*, 1986, *22*, 450–459.

Serbin, L. A., Tonick, I. J., and Sternglanz, S. "Shaping Cooperative Cross-Sex Play." *Child Development*, 1977, *48*, 924–929.

Shaffer, D. R., Pegalis, L., and Cornell, D. P. "Gender and Self-Disclosure Revisited: Personal and Contextual Variations in Self-Disclosure to Same-Sex Acquaintances." *Journal of Social Psychology*, 1992, *132*, 307–315.

Sharabany, R., Gershoni, R., and Hofman, J. E. "Girlfriend, Boyfriend: Age and Sex Differences in Intimate Friendships." *Developmental Psychology*, 1981, *17*, 800–808.

Sheldon, A. "Pickle Fights: Gendered Talk in Preschool Disputes." *Discourse Processes,* 1990, *13,* 5–31.

Sheldon, A. "Conflict Talk: Sociolinguistic Challenges to Self-Assertion and How Young Girls Meet Them." *Merrill-Palmer Quarterly,* 1992, *38,* 95–117.

Sroufe, L. A., Bennett, C., Englund, M., Urban, J., and Shulman, S. "The Significance of Gender Boundaries in Preadolescence: Contemporary Correlates and Antecedents of Boundary Violation and Maintenance." *Child Development,* 1993, *64,* 455–466.

Strayer, F. F., and Strayer, J. "An Ethological Analysis of Social Agonism and Dominance Relations Among Preschool Children." *Child Development,* 1976, *47,* 980–989.

Tannen, D. *You Just Don't Understand: Women and Men in Conversation.* New York: Morrow, 1990.

Thorne, B. "Girls and Boys Together, but Mostly Apart." In W. W. Hartup and Z. Rubin (eds.), *Relationships and Development.* Hillsdale, N.J.: Erlbaum, 1986.

Thorne, B., and Luria, Z. "Sexuality and Gender in Children's Daily Worlds." *Social Problems,* 1986, *33,* 176–190.

Thornton, M. C., Chatters, L. M., Taylor, R. J., and Allen, W. R. "Sociodemographic and Environmental Correlates of Racial Socialization by Black Parents." *Child Development,* 1990, *61,* 401–409.

Weiss, D. M., and Sachs, J. "Persuasive Strategies Used by Preschool Children." *Discourse Processes,* 1991, *14,* 55–72.

West, C., and Zimmerman, D. H. "Gender, Language, and Discourse." In T. A. van Dijk (ed.), *Handbook of Discourse Analysis.* Vol. 4: *Discourse Analysis in Society.* London: Academic Press, 1985.

Whiting, B. B., and Edwards, C. P. *Children of Different Worlds: The Formation of Social Behavior.* Cambridge, Mass.: Harvard University Press, 1988.

Winstead, B. A. "Sex Differences in Same-Sex Friendship." In V. J. Derlega and B. A. Winstead (eds.), *Friendship and Social Interaction.* New York: Springer-Verlag, 1986.

Youniss, J., and Smollar, J. *Adolescents' Relations with Their Mothers, Fathers, and Friends.* Chicago: University of Chicago Press, 1985.

CAMPBELL LEAPER is assistant professor of psychology at the University of California, Santa Cruz.

In an overview of the preceding chapters, the timing of gender segregation, the play style compatibility hypothesis, possible physiological underpinnings, cognitive components in gender differentiation, and the consequences of gender segregation on later development are considered.

Commentary: Gender Segregation in Childhood

Eleanor E. Maccoby

Beginning sometime during the third or fourth year of life, children more and more prefer to play with others of their own sex. This growing preference has been well documented in a wide variety of cultures and settings. What are not well understood are the causes and consequences of this powerful phenomenon of childhood. The chapters in this volume bring us up to date on the relevant research evidence, and present some thoughtful analyses of the developmental sequence of events during the first five years of life that eventuates in the strong gender segregation of middle childhood.

As Beverly Fagot (Chapter Four) warns, we must not fall into the error of assuming that spontaneous cross-sex contact is absent in the school-age years. She cites Gottman's work in showing that some cross-sex friendships are maintained at this time, but that they are usually hidden from the view of peers. Sroufe, Bennett, Englund, Urban, and Shulman, 1993, also discuss the implicit rules observed in the maintenance of gender boundaries by ten- and eleven-year-old children; they argue that children of this age understand that there are certain conditions under which one may interact with children of the other sex and other conditions under which one may not. The gender boundaries are clearly present and are monitored and enforced by peers.

Fagot makes another important point in noting that preschool girls are not only oriented toward other girls but toward adults as well, while boys are more exclusively oriented toward their same-sex peers. Orientation, in this case, includes social proximity and interaction but also means openness to influence. Preschool boys tend to be indifferent to feedback about their behavior from adults and girls, but responsive when the feedback comes from other boys. Girls, by contrast, respond to feedback from all three categories of others: adults, boys, and other girls (Fagot and Leinbach, 1983). Boys tend to be critical of other boys who cross gender boundaries, while girls are quite tolerant toward other girls who show interest in masculine activities. Boys' groups, then, have stronger boundaries than girls' groups, in the sense that they are more self-contained and less permeable by either girls or adults. This difference, as well as segregation itself, is something that needs to be explained.

Timing of Gender Segregation

When do children begin to select same-sex playmates preferentially? The timing of this development is of considerable theoretical interest, since, when we can pinpoint its onset, we can then narrow down the range of possibilities concerning what leads to what. If certain aspects of gender cognition, for example, are usually achieved only after children have begun to congregate in same-sex groups, then these cognitions are not very good candidates for being part of the causal nexus that leads to gender segregation initially.

In toddler playgroups, there is little same-sex preference. At this age, of course, much play is merely parallel. Still, children do display "friendships," in the sense of associating more with certain other children, and Fagot's work with toddlers confirms the earlier reports by Howes (1988) that friendship choices are not gendered at this early age. In the third year, however, same-sex preferences begin to emerge. Fagot has reported that, in one study, "gender segregation evolved slowly over the time period from 18 months to three years, so that by 30 months of age, most children spent the majority of their time with same-sex peers" (Fagot and Leinbach, 1993, p. 6).

LaFreniere, Strayer, and Gauthier (1984) placed the emergence of same-sex preference at about the beginning of the third year. Serbin, Moller, Gulko, Powlishta, and Colburne (Chapter One) began their longitudinal study when the children in their sample were almost three years of age, and followed the children through the ensuing school year. While play in mixed-sex groups was very common, the tendency for children to play more frequently with same-sex than other-sex children was clearly apparent during this year. Furthermore, girls seemed to be taking the lead in establishing same-sex preference. (Girls were also the first to show same-sex preference—or cross-sex avoidance—in the large Canadian day care center studied by LaFreniere, Strayer, and Gauthier.)

Play Style Compatibility Hypothesis

What progress have we made in understanding why this spontaneous segregation of the sexes occurs? One hypothesis has been that the two sexes first develop distinctive play styles, or different preferences for certain toys and activities. They then come to select same-sex playmates because these are the children who are interested in the same toys or activities or whose play styles are especially compatible (see Maccoby and Jacklin, 1987, for a review of studies and hypotheses to that date). The findings reported in several of the chapters in this volume are consistent with the compatibility hypothesis. For example, Fagot finds little or no sex differentiation in play styles or toy preference during the first eighteen months—a time when sex-typed playmate preference is also not seen—but finds that at the end of the second year and continuing into the third, differences in play style and toy preference do emerge. The development of these differences is thus concurrent with the emergence of same-sex playmate preferences, supporting the inference that the two are connected.

Serbin, Moller, Gulko, Powlishta, and Colburne find, however, that three-year-olds who most clearly show same-sex playmate preferences are *not* more likely than nonsegregating children to have sex-typed toy preferences. Maccoby and Jacklin (1987) similarly found no relationship between the masculinity or femininity of a child's toy preferences at forty-five months and the child's tendency to prefer same-sex playmates the following year. The inference is that even though gender-differentiation in toy preferences and differentiation in playmate preferences proceed concurrently, they may not be causally connected.

There is still considerable promise in the compatibility hypothesis, however. Serbin and her colleagues' work suggests that while toy preferences may not matter, play styles do. They found that children with a vigorous, active, physical play style avoided (and probably were also avoided by) children with a quieter play style. Also, children with an adult-oriented play style tended to choose playmates with a similar orientation. That these play-style preferences were reflected in choices of same-sex partners was indicated by the fact that segregating boys were rated by teachers as active and disruptive while segregating girls were rated as high on social sensitivity. When children played in dyads, their play was considerably more interactive with same-sex partners than with other-sex partners; in mixed-sex dyads, both boys and girls engaged in more parallel play and watching than interactive play. This finding fits in nicely with an accumulating body of research pointing to higher levels of interaction in same-sex dyads (Jacklin and Maccoby, 1978; Howes, 1988; Lloyd and Smith, 1986).

Yet Serbin, Moller, Gulko, Powlishta, and Colburne do not accept the compatibility hypothesis unequivocally. The sticking point for them (and for me) is that the play styles of the two sexes do not appear to be particularly differentiated at this early age, at least not in ways that yield mean differences between the sexes on behavioral dimensions usually measured. Serbin and her colleagues cite research showing that, if the social behavior of individual children is aggregated across contexts, neither sex is more sociable, more withdrawn, more aggressive, and so on. It is only when one examines contexts separately—in particular, behavior with same-sex partners compared to that with other-sex partners—that sex differences emerge. Serbin and her colleagues suggest that "children modulate or vary their behavior in different contexts, so that their play is more stimulating when they are with same-sex peers. . . . If so, children might be increasingly drawn to same-sex situations because they find them interesting, stimulating and enjoyable." Differences in interactive styles, they suggest, may emerge *as a result of* continuing experience in same-sex play contexts. Compatibility in play styles then becomes a result, not a cause, of gender segregation, and we are left wondering *why* play is initially more stimulating and interesting with same-sex peers.

Existing evidence seems to me to imply that behavioral compatibility does play a role in children's being initially drawn to same-sex partners, but that once the process begins, play styles in segregated groups progressively differentiate. The rough, active, physical play style of boys remains a good candidate for the feature that initially differentiates the sexes in terms of the kinds of social behaviors that each sex finds attractive or aversive. Boys who are rated by teachers as "disruptive" and/or "active" (Chapter One) or highly "arousable" (Chapter Two) are shown to have especially strong preferences for same-sex playmates. The studies of older children by Bukowski, Gauze, Hoza, and Newcomb (1993) also indicate that it is the boys who especially enjoy rough active play who most often nominate male classmates and least often nominate female classmates as friends. Interestingly, Bukowski and colleagues report that girls who liked rough active play were more likely than other girls to nominate boys as friends. A plausible scenario underlying these preferences is this: a potential play partner approaches vigorously, vocalizing loudly, and seeming to invite chasing or rough play; most girls become wary at such an approach while most boys become pleasantly excited. If boys were initially more likely to make such vigorous approaches to other children, and if boys were also more likely than girls to respond positively to such approaches, we would have identified a bi-directional difference (that is, a sex difference in both the quality of play *initiations* and in the characteristic *response* to certain initiations) that would emerge as a difference in the play styles of dyads (or larger groups). Such a bi-directional difference would clearly be conducive to same-sex partner preference. However, as Serbin and her colleagues say, we need much more information, based on longitudinal observation of children who are in the process of developing a preference for same-sex partners, before we can identify which sex-differentiated social initiations and responses precede and which follow the onset of same-sex preference.

Of crucial importance for the argument is this question: Is a girl made wary by the vigorous approach of *any* potential play partner, regardless of the other child's sex, or only by such an approach from a boy? Is a boy pleasantly excited by the vigorous approach of any child, or only when the approaching child is male? If the latter, our effort at explanation falters, since in that case, we still need to understand why the sex of the other child matters per se, over and above the nature of the behavior that must be responded to.

Possible Physiological Underpinnings

Boys' rough, vigorous play style has often been seen as the prototypical feature that most differentiates the play styles of the two sexes. Can we move one step backward in the explanatory chain and identify physiological processes that might underlie this difference? In Chapter Two, Richard Fabes has explored these possibilities.

Growing out of work with adult male-female couples under varying degrees of stress, Gottman and Levenson (1988) have proposed that males become aroused more easily and more rapidly. Building on this model, Fabes proposes that children's preference for same-sex partners is mediated (at least in part) by sex differences in rates and levels of arousal and perhaps also by differences in how aroused states are regulated. In his review of existing literature, Fabes notes that while it is fairly well established that adult males become more aroused under a variety of stressful conditions, a sex difference in arousal thresholds has by no means been established for children. Although the initial work by Frankenhaeuser (1983) with twelve-year-olds and the early follow-up work by Lundberg (1986) were promising, later work by Lundberg, Westermark, and Rasch (1987), and by Tennes and Kreye (1985), failed to find replicable evidence of sex differences in output of catecholamines in preschoolers and second-graders under a variety of arousing conditions. The work available to date does not resolve the empirical issue, and we must await further studies with new samples in a variety of arousing contexts. Other researchers have studied arousal via measures of cortisol. To date, their findings on sex differences have been largely negative.

Fabes's own work shows that while preschool children of the two sexes did not differ in their levels of arousal under baseline conditions (watching a quiet, relaxing film), boys were more quickly aroused than girls and their arousal dropped off more slowly when the children were exposed to an "evocative" film, namely one in which a child was injured and then teased about the scars. Does this point to a greater arousability in boys in any general sense? Or is there something about the injury and teasing context that especially arouses boys? Fabes suggests the latter, and the literature he cites gives more support to the proposition that boys and girls are aroused by different things than it does to one sex being more generally arousable than the other.

Fabes suggests that girls are responsive to "less evocative" contexts and boys to "highly evocative" ones, but we would need an independent definition of what these levels of evocativeness mean before we can evaluate the hypothesis. Girls are more physiologically aroused than boys by a context that evokes sympathy, but why should we consider such a context less evocative than one that involves danger or conflict (the kind of context that arouses boys more)? What we are left with is the fact that the two sexes differ in the kinds of contexts that they find interesting and exciting. The physiological evidence Fabes provides is helpful in that it is consistent with certain things we already know: for example, that boys are more interested in conflict and danger (as reflected, for example, in the dramatic themes they enact in their play and in their television preferences), while girls are more interested in interpersonal relationships. We could take Fabes's scores as measures of these differing interests. But the physiological measures so far do not add much power to our efforts to explain why these differences exist.

Cognitive Components in Gender Differentiation

The cognitive approach to gender differentiation assigns a causal role to gender cognition. The hypothesis is that knowing the sex identity of self and others and being aware of the stereotypical activities and preferences that are "appropriate" for each sex increases the likelihood that a child will adopt sex-typed behavior. The learning of sex-role stereotypes implies that the learner has already acquired the ability to apply gender labels, since the learner must be able to tag external events with the appropriate label in order to be able to code and organize incoming information according to two major gender categories. Thus, gender-category labeling is fundamental to all the other processes of gender cognition and underlies the formation of superordinate gender schemas (Chapter Three). We know that once a gender-category label is applied, inferences are readily made by four-year-olds concerning distinctive characteristics of members of the two groups, while inferring gender-category membership from distinctive properties comes later (Gelman, Collman, and Maccoby, 1986).

The fund of gender-related information may include prescriptive knowledge, that is, knowing not only how members of each sex do behave, but how they are *expected to* behave. These two kinds of knowledge are not necessarily acquired at the same time. For example, it is possible for a child to know that boys like to play with trucks and girls with dolls without believing that they *ought*, or are expected, to do so. Indeed, as Damon's early work (1977) indicated, children of kindergarten age may not believe that there is anything wrong with a child's playing with toys usually reserved for the other sex, even though they are aware of which toys are "boys' toys" and which are normally "for girls." Damon found that it was only in the early grade-school years that this knowledge took on a prescriptive quality. Clearly, differential reactions by parents or peers to sex-appropriate versus sex-inappropriate behavior on a child's part may affect the child's behavior directly, whether or not the child has cognition of external sanctions. Probably, differential reactions by social partners shape children's sex-typed behavior considerably earlier than the age at which children can report what behavior elicits the approval or disapproval of others. Nevertheless, it is of some interest to discover at what age children become aware of the reward and punishment contingencies that prevail in their environment, and to see whether such awareness adds to their adoption of stereotypical behavior.

As Carol Martin says (Chapter Four), gender schemas are presumed not only to guide behavior directly but to constitute a filter that affects the intake, organization, and retention of gender-relevant information. It is a subordinate own-sex schema that presumably directs this task. Gender stereotypical knowledge becomes tagged with an additional label on one of the categories that indicates "same as me" or "relevant to me." Martin proposes that gender knowledge included in the own-sex schema is more differentiated and detailed than that in the other-sex schema. The core of the own-sex schema, we may assume, is the individual's knowledge of his or her own gender category, and this knowledge probably results in more than its simply forming the core of a self-schema. Gender identity is something in which children become invested in some broader sense. At a certain point, children become indignant if others mistake their gender. And, as Carol Martin notes, formation of the own-sex schema sets in motion certain group processes, such as valuing more highly the characteristics of one's own group and devaluing those of the out-group.

The splitting off and differentiation of the own-sex schema is presumed to have motivational consequences. That is, children may observe and learn differences in the social roles and behavior of male and female persons, but as Kohlberg (1966) suggested many years ago, this will have no personal relevance to them until their gender knowledge is linked to their gender identity. Once they know their own sex and that of others, the theory says, they become motivated to put their gender knowledge to work, that is, to adapt their own behavior to what they have learned is appropriate for their sex. But not only does the importance of gender knowledge depend on the formation of gender identity, the reverse is also true. That is, without knowledge of gender stereotypes, the acquisition of gender identity would have little effect, since no matter how motivated a gender-identified child might be to behave appropriately for his or her own sex, the effort would be fruitless without a sex-differentiated template the child could adapt to.

To what extent do existing data support a causal role for gender cognitions in the development of same-sex partner preferences? Let us consider first the timetable for gender cognitions. It seems to be approximately as follows: perceptual categorizing comes first. Infants can discriminate between male and female persons (at least, between the pictures and voices of adult men and women) by around the end of the first year. Correct gender labeling of self and others comes next, toward the middle or end of the third year. It is roughly concurrent with the development of gender segregation. A good deal of knowledge concerning the toy and activity preference of children of each sex is in place by age four, and children's knowledge extends beyond the simply factual into the realm of metaphor. Hort and Leinbach (1993) have documented that an object to which threatening or dark features have been added (for example, black paint or spikes or large teeth) is more likely to be labeled "for boys" by children of both sexes. By age four, children also know something about the sex-typing of adult occupational roles. Gender stereotypes are greatly expanded and consolidated in the ensuing years, and scores on standard tests of sex-role knowledge (for example, the Sex Role Learning Index (SERLI); see Serbin, Powlishta, and Gulko, 1993) reach a ceiling by age seven. It is important to note that the acquisition of gender knowledge does not appear to be sex-differentiated, at least with respect to the measures usually used. Thus, even though cognitive theory would lead us to expect that children would be especially interested in selecting and be primed to remember information more relevant to their own sex, tests of children's information have so far not shown this selective bias.

Knowledge of the distinctive traits of the two sexes develops much more slowly. It is striking that the four- to six-year-olds studied by Martin and her colleagues showed quite weak knowledge of the play styles prevailing in boys' as compared to girls' groups. For example, few believed that fighting or chasing was more common among boys or that playing indoors and being helpful was more common among girls. It is especially interesting that such knowledge was particularly weak concerning children of the other sex. Thus, children of each sex showed relatively little knowledge of the other-sex characteristics that would presumably make play with other-sex partners seem potentially incompatible. It may be, of course, that a broader sampling of traits would yield stronger results: children may know that play is rougher among boys even if they may not believe that boys characteristically fight or chase.

This timetable tells us something about possible cognitive contributions to gender segregation. Although play style compatibility may be directly implicated in getting same-sex playmate preferences under way, it would appear that it is not necessary for children to conceptualize the sex differences in play styles in order to respond to them. Gender segregation is well under way considerably before children appear to be aware of play style differences. Being able to label the sex of self and others, however, may be a necessary or at least facilitating condition for choosing playmates on the basis of their gender. There is some evidence for this linkage in Fagot's work, cited by Martin, that shows that early labelers are also among the first children to show same-sex playmate preferences.

Martin reviews the evidence concerning the relationship between gender knowledge and same-sex partner preference and finds that the two appear to have little or no connection. This finding is consistent with work on sex-typed toy preferences, which also indicates that these preferences do not depend on children's having acquired knowledge of what toys are sex-appropriate (see Bussey and Bandura, 1992, for a recent example). Bussey and Bandura suggest that children do develop personal standards for gender-relevant behavior and, at age four, have come to regulate their own behavior on the basis of these standards, but Bussey and Bandura also suggest that this comes *after* the child has already adopted sex-typed behavior for other reasons. Such findings, they suggest, do not support the idea that children are striving to match their behavior to what they understand to be sex-appropriate, at least not in the initial phases of behavioral sex-differentiation. This analysis appears to be equally valid for the preference for same-sex playmates: at the time this preference develops, it is not related to the level of children's general knowledge about gender stereotypes. There is one kind of knowledge that might be particularly relevant to gender segregation, and that is some level of awareness concerning the attitudes of peers about cross-sex play. There is considerable evidence that peers do monitor and sanction one another's behavior from preschool age onward—this process being considerably more active and potent among boys than girls—but as noted earlier, it is possible that explicit knowledge of the contingencies might add to peers' power. This possibility has been largely ignored in research to date, and Martin makes a contribution by incorporating children's awareness of their peers' reactions into her studies. In her data, this factor emerges as possibly important. Children who believed that "other kids like it" if they played with same-sex peers were more likely to express same-sex playmate preferences. However, more work is needed to discover whether children's awareness of such social contingencies affects mainly their verbally reported preferences or their overt sex-typed behavior as well. In particular, it would be important to find out whether the effectiveness of external contingencies is enhanced by children's being explicitly aware of them.

In summary, the ability to apply gender labels to other persons may be important in gender segregation. On the whole, however, early same-sex partner preferences do not appear to depend on the more comprehensive gender schemas that encompass children's fund of gender-stereotyped information. We should be aware, however, that much of the work on gender cognition has been focused on cognitions that might affect children's adoption of sex-typed toy or activity preferences rather than their preference for same-sex playmates. The two may not have the same cognitive underpinnings. Furthermore, even though the contributions of gender cognitions to same-sex playmate preferences may be minimal in the third and fourth years of life when gender segregation gets under way, there is every reason to believe that these cognitions do strengthen same-sex preferences later, when more active processes of self-regulation, based on standards that are part of cognition, come into play.

Consequences of Gender Segregation

The contributors to this volume ask not only why gender segregation occurs, but what difference it makes. Campbell Leaper, in particular (Chapter Five), focuses on the second question. One consequence of gender segregation has been widely noted: male and female playgroups develop different kinds of interpersonal skills within their segregated groups and different group agendas. Leaper argues that the play styles that develop within boys' and girls' playgroups foster different styles of relating. Girls in their groups acquire social sensitivity, which fosters their achievement of interpersonal closeness. Boys' playgroups, Leaper suggests, with their emphasis on competition and dominance, constitute a social milieu in which individual assertion, more than affiliation, is fostered. Leaper notes that boys' groups are by no means mere collections of self-asserting individuals: they have overarching group goals and cooperate "in a competitive mode" to achieve these goals. But Leaper assigns the learning of skills for "coordinating one's personal interests with those of others" mainly to girls' groups. I would suggest that learning to coordinate personal goals with the goals of others is equally important in boys' groups, and that we sometimes underestimate the role of male peer groups in moderating and channelling individual self-assertion. Leaper is undoubtedly right, however, in stressing that the maintenance of interpersonal harmony is a more important part of girls' than boys' group agendas. And his own research with college students gives further depth to the meaning of intimacy and reciprocity in female pairs: while men in male pairs proved themselves to be entirely capable of self-disclosure when placed in a situation that called for it, male partners did not support self-disclosures. However, in female pairs, self-disclosures were responded to with active understanding.

In discussing the fact that boys appear to be more active than girls in the maintenance of gender-group boundaries, Leaper raises an issue that is central to our understanding of gender differentiation: the relative social status of the two sexes. It remains a question whether girls accord higher status to male groups; in fact, girls commonly disapprove of what they see as boys' "wild" or "mean" characteristics, just as boys derogate girls for their lack of toughness. Society as a whole may accord greater status to boys' groups, although—at least at the present time—there is reason to doubt whether people in general value stereotypically male characteristics (for example, independence, assertiveness, dominance) more highly than female ones (intimacy, reciprocity, empathy). Still there may be a certain recognition, among children and adults alike, that boys' groups need to be taken more seriously. They tend to be larger, and more of their activities are countercultural, so that boys in groups become more threatening than boys taken singly. Leaper means more than this, however, when he talks about the social status of the two groups. He suggests that the maintenance of boundaries between the two groups is part and parcel of the more pervasive social processes that create and maintain sex differences in status.

If this hypothesis is correct, it has wide implications. Earlier, I suggested that male peer groups probably have useful functions, a major one being the moderation and channelling of male aggression and assertiveness. Positive sequelae from girls' experiences in their peer groups have also been claimed. And the current resurgence of advocacy for single-sex schools argues that girls experience a better learning environment if their classrooms are free of male dominance. However, if gender segregation in childhood also sustains or even strengthens the status differential between the sexes, then it runs counter to what many of us see as an essential requirement for adaptation to the modern world: the weakening of gendered status distinctions in all aspects of our lives—the occupational, the political, and the domestic. Leaper suggests ways whereby parents and teachers can support cooperative cross-sex interaction among children. It remains to be seen whether we can have our cake and eat it too; that is, enable children to profit from the lessons best learned in same-sex peer groups, while at the same time sustaining our progress toward gender equity through childhood and into adulthood.

References

Bukowski, W. H., Gauze, C., Hoza, B., and Newcomb, A. F. "Differences and Consistency Between Same-Sex and Other-Sex Peer Relationships During Early Adolescence." *Developmental Psychology*, 1993, *29,* 255–263.

Bussey, K., and Bandura, A. "Self-Regulatory Mechanisms Governing Gender Development." *Child Development,* 1992, *63* (5), 1236–1250.

Damon, W. *The Social World of the Child.* San Francisco: Jossey- Bass, 1977.

Fagot, B. I., and Leinbach, M. D. "Play Styles in Early Childhood: Social Consequences for Boys and Girls." In M. B. Liss (ed.), *Social and Cognitive Skills: Sex Roles and Children's Play.* San Diego: Academic Press, 1983.

Fagot, B. I., and Leinbach, M. D. "Gender-Role Development in Young Children: From Discrimination to Labeling." *Developmental Review,* 1993, *13* (2), 205–224.

Frankenhaeuser, M. "The Sympathetic-Adrenal and Pituitary-Adrenal Response to Challenge: Comparison Between the Sexes." In T. M. Dembroski, T. H. Schmidt, and G. Blumchen (eds.), *Biobehavioral Bases of Coronary Heart Disease.* New York: Karger, 1983.

Gelman, S. A., Collman, P., and Maccoby, E. E. "Inferring Properties from Categories Versus Inferring Categories from Properties: The Case of Gender." *Child Development,* 1986, *57* (2), 396–404.

Gottman, J. M., and Levenson, R. W. "The Social Psychophysiology of Marriage." In P. Noller and M. A. Fitzpatrick (eds.), *Perspectives on Marital Interaction.* Philadelphia: Multilingual Matters, 1988.

Hort, E., and Leinbach, M. D. "Children's Use of Metaphorical Cues in Gender-Typing of Objects." Paper presented at the 60th anniversary meeting of the Society for Research in Child Development, New Orleans, Mar. 1993.

Howes, C. "Peer Interaction of Young Children." *Monographs of the Society for Research in Child Development,* 1988, *53* (1).

Jacklin, C. N., and Maccoby, E. E. "Social Behavior at 33 Months in Same-Sex and Mixed-Sex Dyads." *Child Development,* 1978, *49,* 557–569.

Kohlberg, L. "A Cognitive-Developmental Analysis of Children's Sex Role Concepts and Attitudes." In E. E. Maccoby (ed.), *The Development of Sex Differences.* Stanford, Calif.: Stanford University Press, 1966.

LaFreniere, P., Strayer, F. F., and Gauthier, R. "The Emergence of Same-Sex Affiliative Preferences Among Preschool Peers: A Developmental/Ethological Perspective." *Child Development,* 1984, *55,* 1958–1965.

Lloyd, B., and Smith, C. "The Effects of Age and Gender on Social Behavior in Very Young Children." *British Journal of Social Psychology,* 1986, *25,* 33–41.

Lundberg, U. "Stress and Type A Behavior in Children." *Journal of the American Academy of Child Psychiatry,* 1986, *25* (6), 771–778.

Lundberg, U., Westermark, O., and Rasch, B. *Type A Behavior and Physiological Stress Responses in Preschool Children: Sex Differences at the Ages of Three and Four.* Reports from the Department of Psychology, University of Stockholm, #664. Stockholm: Department of Psychology, University of Stockholm, Nov. 1987.

Maccoby, E. E., and Jacklin, C. N. "Gender Segregation in Childhood." In H. Reese (ed.), *Advances in Child Behavior and Development.* Vol. 20. San Diego: Academic Press, 1987.

Serbin, L. A., Powlishta, K. K., and Gulko, J. "The Development of Sex Typing in Middle Childhood." *Monographs of the Society for Research in Child Development,* 1993, *58* (2, Serial 232).

Sroufe, L. A., Bennett, C., Englund, M., Urban, J., and Shulman, S. "The Significance of Gender Boundaries in Preadolescence: Contemporary Correlates and Antecedents of Boundary Violation and Maintenance." *Child Development,* 1993, *64* (2), 455–466.

Tennes, K., and Kreye, M. "Children's Adrenocortical Responses to Classroom Activities and Tests in Elementary School." *Psychosomatic Medicine,* 1985, *47,* 451–460.

ELEANOR E. MACCOBY is the Barbara Kimball Browning Professor (emerita) of Developmental Psychology, Stanford University.

NAME INDEX

Subject Index

Abstract gender theories, 40–41
Academic achievement, 3
Adrenaline, 21
Adults, girls' interactions with, 58, 60, 63, 87
Affiliation: exhibited in sex-typed play, 68; in females, 70; in males, 71
Age, gender differences in arousability and, 31–32
Aggression: in less-secure males, 56; male stereotype and, 54; social, 71
Arousability. *See* Emotional arousability
Assertion: as element of collaborative social interaction strategy, 70; exhibited in sex-typed play, 68
Attachment theory, 56, 57

Behavioral compatibility theory: emergence of gender segregation and, 38, 55; explanation of, 2, 54, 88–89; maintenance and strengthening of gender segregation and, 41–42; play styles and role of, 90; toddlers and, 10
Block play, 61–62
Borderwork: asymmetries in, 73; explanation of, 72
Boys: aggression in less-secure, 56; physiological reactivity in infant, 20–21; response to stress, 21, 24; sex-typed play in, 68, 69

Cognitive development, 58–62
Cognitive-developmental theory: gender identity and, 8, 13; problems with, 55
Collaborative social interaction strategy, 70
Competition: interpersonal closeness and, 70–71; seen in male social interaction styles, 19, 69–70
Coping modes, 24
Cortisol, 21
Cross-sex peer relations: asymmetries in borderwork and, 73; conditions for, 87; in-group identity and, 72–73; intimacy and, 74–76; physical appearance, attractiveness and, 73–74; social influence strategies, male dominance and, 71–72

Dependency, 56
Dominance hierarchies: cross-sex peer relations and, 72; female avoidance of male, 19; within male peer groups, 69, 70; rough-and-tumble play and, 26–27

Emotional arousability: ability to influence and, 25–27; context and, 23–24; emotional intensity and threshold of, 22–23; establishment of female-male differences in, 20–25; gender segregation and, 27–32; play and playgroup preferences and, 28, 91; social behaviors and perceptions of others and, 21–22; sociometric judgments and, 29; variations in ability to regulate, 24–25, 91
Emotional development, 58, 59
Emotional intensity, 22–23
Emotional reactivity: differences in, 2; regulation through allocation of attention, 23–24
Emotion-focused coping, 24

Families, segregation of males from females within, 53

Gender boundary maintenance: asymmetries in, 73; explanation of, 72; male maintenance of, 96
Gender cognitions: causal role of, 92, 93; same-sex peer preferences and, 2
Gender cultures approach, 1
Gender differentiation: cognitive components in, 92–95; contextual phenomena and, 8–9, 25; emphasis placed on, 1
Gender identity: cognitive theory and, 8, 13; importance placed on, 93; in segregated vs. nonsegregated children, 14
Gender knowledge: abstract, 37; changes in, 42–43; development of, 94; explicit, 36–37; exploration of, 46–47; tests of, 55
Gender labels: ability to apply, 95; influence of, 39–40; results of knowledge of, 54–55
Gender schema theories: gender concept formation and, 72; variations among, 36

103

Ordering Information

New Directions for Child Development is a series of paperback books that presents the latest research findings on all aspects of children's psychological development, including their cognitive, social, moral, and emotional growth. Books in the series are published quarterly in Fall, Winter, Spring, and Summer and are available for purchase by subscription and individually.

Subscriptions for 1994 cost $54.00 for individuals (a savings of 25 percent over single-copy prices) and $75.00 for institutions, agencies, and libraries. Please do not send institutional checks for personal subscriptions. Standing orders are accepted.

Single copies cost $17.95 when payment accompanies order. (California, New Jersey, New York, and Washington, D.C., residents please include appropriate sales tax.) All orders will be charged postage and handling.

Discounts for quantity orders are available. Please write to the address below for information.

All orders must include either the name of an individual or an official purchase order number. Please submit your order as follows:
  Subscriptions: specify series and year subscription is to begin
  Single copies: include individual title code (such as CD59)

Mail all orders to:
  Jossey-Bass Publishers
  350 Sansome Street
  San Francisco, California 94104-1342

For subscription sales outside of the United States, contact any international subscription agency or Jossey-Bass directly.